T0126094

ELIZABETH DAVID'S CHRISTMAS

Elizabeth David's
CHRISTMAS

Edited by Jill Norman

FOREWORD BY ALICE WATERS

ILLUSTRATED BY MARY ROSS

DAVID R. GODINE · PUBLISHER
BOSTON

First US edition published in 2008 by
DAVID R. GODINE · *Publisher*
Post Office Box 450
Jaffrey, New Hampshire 03452
www.godine.com

Copyright © 2003 The Estate of Elizabeth David and Jill Norman
Foreword copyright © 2008 Alice Waters
Illustrations copyright © 2008 Mary Ross

First published in Great Britain in 2003
by Penguin Books Ltd, London

All rights reserved.
No part of this book may be used or reproduced in any manner
whatsoever without written permission from the publisher, except
in the case of brief excerpts embodied in critical articles and reviews.
For information contact Permissions, David R. Godine, Publisher,
15 Court Square, Suite 320, Boston, Massachusetts, 02108.

LIBRARY OF CONGRESS CATALOGING-IN-PUBLICATION DATA
David, Elizabeth, 1913–1992.
Elizabeth David's Christmas / edited by Jill Norman. — 1st ed.
p.   cm.
Includes bibliographical references and index.
ISBN 978-1-56792-361-2 (hardcover)
ISBN 978-1-56792-558-6 (softcover)
1. Christmas cookery. I. Norman, Jill. II. Title. III. Title: Christmas.
TX739.2.C45D38 2008
641.5'686—dc22
2008028677

FIRST SOFTCOVER EDITION
Printed in The United States of America

Contents

FOREWORD

THIS IS Elizabeth David at her most delightful: recipes, history, anecdotes, quotations, and opinions, all in her bracing lucid prose. To read it is to be reminded that she was among the very best writers about food of all time. With Jill Norman as her editor, Elizabeth's legacy has the perfect steward: someone who was also a uniquely knowledgeable and devoted personal friend.

I am one of those who was touched by Elizabeth David's writings at an early and impressionable age, when I was a struggling graduate student in London in the nineteen-sixties. I read everything she wrote that I could get my hands on and cooked every recipe of hers I could manage on the hot plate in my tiny room. (I still have some of those yellowing Penguin paperbacks, dog-eared and stained with olive oil, with my penciled exclamation points in the margins.) To me she was the champion of simplicity and beauty in the kitchen, the defender of the authentic and the seasonal, and the ultimate arbiter of taste and proportion. I so internalized her influence that it comes as no great surprise that many of the Christmas traditions that evolved in my own family are echoes of the themes in this book.

Having decided to forego the exchange of gifts and collaborate instead on a feast, my family for many years chose a country we all wanted to visit and prepared a Christmas celebration accordingly, cooking a Provençal Christmas Eve supper one year and a Mexican one the next, and a Sicilian one the year after, drawing on many occasions from Elizabeth's books. This Christmas book makes me regret a little that we never attempted an all-out English Christmas dinner. You could not ask for a more clear-headed account of the care you have to take to properly achieve one. (A reviewer of the British edition of this book complained that the recipes lacked "short-cuts" — as if this were a drawback and not an inspiration!)

Elizabeth David was incapable of dishonesty, and one of the most delightfully quirky things about her Christmas book is its frankness. She is unafraid to say that she hasn't made a Christmas pudding in thirty-five years and hopes to never make another, but she follows this with instructions for doing so that are so comprehensive and so fascinating that you will be sorely tempted to try and make one yourself. Elizabeth knew that Christmas is a holiday fraught with ambiguities, and she is perhaps at her most lovable when, having acknowledged that Christmas is the quintessential family holiday, she expresses her unfulfilled wish to be left alone instead, in bed, with a tray of smoked salmon and a glass of Champagne.

This year my daughter and I will celebrate a merry Christmas the same way we have the last few years, in a manner which owes a lot to Elizabeth, and of which I am pretty sure she would have approved: I will have boiled and baked a ham to have on hand for a few days, but we won't have a throng of friends and relatives around the table. That's what Thanksgiving is for. Instead we will get up quietly on Christmas morning; I will rekindle the fire in the kitchen and bake some soda bread in the fireplace, in a cast-iron Dutch oven; and the two of us will eat it with nothing else but sweet butter, smoked salmon, a little salad, and, sure enough, an icy cold bottle of Champagne. And we'll drink to the memory of Elizabeth David.

ALICE WATERS

October 2008

PREFACE

I REMEMBER A TIME one January when Elizabeth first talked about putting together articles and recipes for a book that was to be called *Food for Christmas*. She had had more than the usual number of requests from friends and family for forgotten recipes and had decided that it was time to gather all her material on cooking for Christmas into a small book. This was back in the seventies. We agreed on the style and content: recipes, both conventional and unconventional; essays describing some aspect of Christmas; extracts and quotations from other writers.

Time passed, the pressures remembered from the previous Christmas dwindled, and other projects took precedence. From time to time we discussed the idea again, but always inconclusively. I was very surprised, therefore, to discover, in the last box of papers to be sorted out after her death, that there was a substantial Christmas file. In it were all of the articles and recipes she had written in her years as a journalist, a list of other recipes to be included from the published books, a few cuttings from other writers, and an introduction. Had I known all those years ago that so much work had been done, I would have put more pressure on Elizabeth to finish the book. I have put it together now in the spirit that Elizabeth intended, with her introduction, the recipes and the articles that still have an interest today.

The style of the recipes varies, as Elizabeth's writing changed over the years. The early recipes tend to be quite short, whereas later ones are often accompanied by explanatory notes. The recipes for cured meats call for saltpeter, which, unfortunately, pharmacists are no longer permitted to sell. The best solution is to find a friendly local butcher who pickles his own meat and ask if he will supply some. If you can't get it, you can cure the meat without it, for the purpose of saltpeter is not preservative but cosmetic: it gives the meat its appetizing pink color.

Elizabeth was very familiar with the need of most cooks to provide enough food to see a large family through several days' meals and snacks and found solutions to simplify and reduce the amount of preparation and cooking. For many years she helped with the Christmas preparations for her sister's family; later in her life she chose to spend Christmas Day quietly at home doing very little cooking at all, with some simple food and a good bottle of wine. On Boxing Day, which was her birthday, she enjoyed going out, sometimes to lunch with our family, sometimes with other friends, or occasionally she entertained a few friends at home. Her complaints about the commercialization of Christmas are even more relevant today than when she wrote them; the frenzy of shopping and cooking is no less. I imagine that a lot of cooks will envy Elizabeth's choice of "smoked salmon, home-made bread, butter, lovely cold white Alsace wine" as "a glorious way to celebrate Christmas" as they make their own more complex preparations. I hope that her practical advice and simple recipes will help them take the strain out of cooking over the holidays.

JILL NORMAN

July 2003

INTRODUCTION

CHRISTMAS COMES but once a year. Don't ever say that to a cookery journalist. Cookery journalists know different. For them, three times a year would be nearer the mark. First, around mid-August, when they must start work on the recipes, at any rate if they contribute regularly to a glossy monthly. There'll probably be color photographs to cook for and supervise as well. The next round comes about the end of September when the article has to be written and something original – well, anyway different from last year – dredged up in the way of advice about the turkey and the leftovers. The third time it actually is Christmas, when it's all cooked for real, although not without notes being made for next year's stint. In between delivery of the monthly article there will almost certainly be another couple of Christmas pieces to write, for a weekly, a wine merchant's newsletter, a Sunday, a daily.

From 1949 to 1964 I was cookery contributor to quite a variety of publications and collected a fairly bulky file of recipes and articles relating to Christmas. It all started with nearly seven years on *Harper's Bazaar* followed by four or five – to run concurrently as judges say when delivering sentence – on *Vogue, Vogue House and Garden* – a monthly article for each – and the *Sunday Times* (that was in the far-off days before the color supplement). In the early sixties it was the *Sunday Despatch,* for a brief period the *Daily Telegraph,* then the *Spectator,* whose editors happily didn't require recipes, and the *Wine and Food Society's Quarterly,* under the editorship of Hugh Johnson who did. At the same time there were miscellaneous articles for wine merchants, Harrods' food catalogues, and other publications I have now forgotten. One year I put together about ten of the recipes that had become established favorites and gave copies to my sisters and one or two friends who invariably telephoned three days before Christmas to say that the recipe for Cumberland sauce was mislaid, or somebody had borrowed the page with the timing for the turkey and not returned it, so could I please read the instructions over the telephone. Need I say it, before too long not one of these little files of recipes could be found, and by now the sons and daughters of my sisters and friends were asking for the recipes their mothers used. This time I'm getting all the recipes together and putting them between the covers of a little book, not so easily mislaid, I hope, as those files of long ago.

Some of the recipes collected together here have, of course, appeared in other books of mine. Between 1950 and 1970 I published six volumes of cookery, so it was inevitable that Christmas recipes should find their way into two or three of them. As reminders, I think it will be useful to have them all under one roof, as it were. I had myself forgotten for example how wonderfully good and useful I used to find some of the old French recipes that I included in an article on Christmas dishes and menus in France. These were subsequently published in *French Provincial Cooking*. An almond and orange cake from *Mediterranean Food* was at one time a steady during the days when I helped out my sister Diana Grey with the Christmas cooking for her family of five young children. Later this cake was superseded by an Italian chocolate one. (Rich fruit cakes never figured in my Christmas cooking, nor in my sister's. The children didn't really like them, and we ourselves had had rather too much of them when we were children. The same went for the Christmas pudding.) At a still later stage my sister turned the chocolate cake into a chocolate ice cream. That was one of the great treats of her children's Christmas. One of her sons still makes it every year. So, although it doesn't sound very Christmassy, I've included the recipe here.

For Christmas 1958, my *Vogue* article introduced, or rather revived, the beautiful dry-spiced beef of eighteenth-century England. This recipe and several others for Christmas cold meats published in the same article were reprinted in my 1970 Penguin, *Spices, Salt and Aromatics in the English Kitchen.* They reappear here. The article which introduced them is also reprinted here. Several more introductory pieces from those *Vogue* and *House and Garden* days of the late fifties also reappear here, as do a few recipes and extracts from the *Wine and Food Quarterly.* The article dealing with the Christmas hampers of the early sixties was originally written for the *Spectator.* An article I enjoyed writing was the 1964 *Spectator* one describing late autumn and the pre-Christmas preparations in southeastern Spain, "*Para Navidad.*"

If here and there in my account of a cookery journalist's Christmases a note of desperation is clearly audible, I don't make apologies. Christmas, at any rate the way we are supposed to celebrate it nowadays, does tend to unbalance people, particularly those people responsible for the catering, the cooking, the presents, the tree, the decorations. There are times indeed when it's difficult not to regret the failure of the Cromwell regime's bid to suppress the whole thing. Clandestine festivities would have been a lot more fun and have infinitely more meaning than today's enforced jollifications, and perhaps the lovely carols and the church services might have retained their prime importance in the Christmas celebration instead of taking very much second place to the cooking, the meal, the exchange of presents, the sovereign's speech on television.

Commercial interests being what they are, however, we are unlikely, in any foreseeable future, to be spared the annual orgy of spending, the jammed streets, the frantic shoppers in the stores, the whole circus of what Hugh Johnson once described as the season of the Great Too Much. I'd better leave it, I think, at that – adding only that, since Hugh threw out that ominous little phrase, it's also become the Great Too Long. A ten-day shut-down, no less, is now normal at Christmas. On at least one day during the Great Too Long Stretch I stay in bed, making myself lunch on a tray. Smoked salmon, home-made bread, butter, lovely cold white Alsace wine. A glorious way to celebrate Christmas.

ELIZABETH DAVID

ELIZABETH DAVID'S CHRISTMAS

Roses are things which Christmas is not a bed of.
OGDEN NASH

Celebrating Christmas

CHRISTMAS IS A FAMILY OCCASION

· I ·

CHRISTMAS IS A family occasion. On that point few English people would disagree. In my family the occasion always amounted also to something rather more than the celebration of Christmas. This was due to the circumstance of so many of us having birthdays at the same season, a season that opened on December 9th with my younger sister Diana's birthday. On December 18th came my mother's turn. On the 26th and 27th came respectively my own and my elder sister's celebrations. When we grew up that elder sister married a man who was born on the 28th. Later my younger sister's only daughter chose to appear on the 19th. (Her four sons were decently spaced, thank heaven, throughout the spring, summer and autumn.)

For us as children, then, Christmas meant a period of present-giving, birthday cakes, candles and crackers prolonged to the point of satiety and beyond. After the Christmas stockings – four of them for my mother to get ready – the Christmas pudding, the cake, the mince pies, came my birthday cake. Next day my elder sister's. In those days we lived in a big house, with domestic staff and a cook who made the cakes. At teatime,

[3]

the birthday child of the day was sent down to the kitchen bearing slices of the celebration cake, offering them all round, thanking cook, kitchen maid, scullery maid, anyone who happened to be around, for the lovely cake, repeating the season's greetings, returning to the tea table for second helpings, to be released at last back to the nursery, our presents, Nannie and bed – come along now all of you, come along, you've had enough excitement for one day.

When I was ten, my father died. After that everything was different. We spent Christmases with cousins in Hampshire, sons and daughters of my mother's only sister. Their house was much larger and grander than ours. There were five children of our own ages, and usually another family of four young cousins, children of my mother's younger brother. In the general Christmas carry-on, the preparations, the making of the paper chains, the gilding of walnuts to hang on one huge tree for the family, another for the village hall, prayers every morning followed by full-dress country-house breakfasts, long lunches – turkeys, hams with delicious Cumberland sauce – the distractions provided by aunts, uncles, older cousins and all our contemporaries, crackers, carols, snapdragon, a good deal of church, our own embarrassing birthdays seemed to pass almost unnoticed. I, for one, was thankful. All the same, Christmas was still, for the rather withdrawn child I had become, a trial.

It wasn't really until the days of wartime work in Egypt with the Admiralty and subsequently the Ministry of Information that I was able to do what I pleased at Christmas. Liberated from family ties and birthday celebrations, busy with office work, usually on duty on Christmas morning and again in the evening, I could all the same manage a small lunch party, stopping on my way home from the office to gather up an old friend who might otherwise have been spending a lonely Christmas. One of those Christmas lunches in my little Cairo flat I remember well. There was no time for Christmas decorations and food was fairly basic. But someone had given me a NAAFI Christmas pudding and I had explained to my cook Suleiman how to pour warmed brandy over it and set it alight as he brought it to the table. There was no more than a meter between kitchen and diningroom. There could hardly, I supposed, be a problem. What I had overlooked was precise instruction as to the moment to bring in the pudding. Suleiman had never previously worked for English people. It was hardly surprising then that after the omelettes, which had made a modest start to our festive meal, Suleiman proudly bore in the blazing pudding. In consternation I asked him if some disaster had overtaken the turkey. No, no. That would come next. The time for the pudding satisfactorily explained, I thought, it was taken away and the turkey brought on. (Egyptian turkeys were bred in the Fayoum district. They were small but good.) Instead of vegetables the pudding was once more presented. Eventually, by the time the proper moment for it actually arrived, that pudding had already made three entrances, each time splendidly ablaze. No wonder. Nearly a whole bottle of Egyptian brandy had contributed to the fireworks. The pudding was tipsy. So, by the time we had eaten it, were we. To the point when we all agreed that it was the finest Christmas pudding we had ever eaten. Quite an achievement for a NAAFI pudding and a wartime one at that. On the whole I doubt if there are many Christmas meals I've enjoyed quite as much as that absurd lunch in my cramped little orange-box of a flat across the road from the Nile. As for Suleiman, I said no more about the pudding. How was it possible at that stage to explain to a Berber from the

Sudan that that astonishing concoction with its ritual flames was neither meat nor vegetable nor bird nor cake but simply the obligatory English Christmas dessert?

UNTRADITIONAL CHRISTMAS FOOD

IF I HAD MY WAY – and I shan't – my Christmas Day eating and drinking would consist of an omelette and cold ham and a nice bottle of wine at lunchtime, and a smoked salmon sandwich with a glass of champagne on a tray in bed in the evening. This lovely, selfish, anti-gorging, un-Christmas dream of hospitality, either given or taken, must be shared by thousands of women who know it's all Lombard Street to a China orange that they'll spend both Christmas Eve and Christmas morning peeling, chopping, mixing, boiling, roasting, steaming. That they will eat and drink too much, that someone will say the turkey isn't quite as good as last year, or discover that the rum for the pudding has been forgotten, that by the time lunch has been washed up and put away it'll be teatime, not to say drink or dinner time, and tomorrow it's the weekend, and it's going to start all over again.

Well, I know that any woman who has to provide for a lot of children or a big family has no alternative. The grisly orgy of spending and cooking and anxiety has to be faced. We are so many fathoms deep in custom and tradition and sentiment over Christmas; we have got so far, with our obsessive present-buying and frenzied cooking, from the spirit of a simple Christian festival, that only the most determined of Scrooges can actually turn their faces to the wall and ignore the whole thing when the time comes. All the same, there must be quite a few small families, couples without children, and people living alone, who like to celebrate Christmas in a reasonably modest and civilized way: inviting just a friend or two who might otherwise also be alone (well, maybe, like you and me, they'd rather *be* alone, but this is an eccentricity not accepted at Christmas time) – and for such small-scale Christmas meals at least the shopping and cooking marathons can be avoided, the host and hostess can be allowed to enjoy themselves, and the guests needn't have guilt about the washing-up.

For such a meal, I'd make the main dish something fairly straightforward and conventional, the color and the festive look being supplied by something bright and beautiful as a garnish. Not inedible decorations, but something simple and unexpected such as a big bowl of crimson sweet-sour cherry sauce with a roast duck; a handsome dish of tomatoes stuffed with savory rice with a capon; a Madeira and truffle-scented sauce with a piece of plain roast beef; sliced oranges with a pork roast or a ham.

The first course I'd make as painless as possible for the cook: if money were no object, lots of smoked salmon or Parma ham to precede the duck; before the beef, a French duck pâté with truffles and pistachio nuts, avocado pears, or simply a lovely dish of egg or prawn mayonnaise. Or, if you'd cooked a ham or piece of gammon or pickled pork to last over the Christmas holiday, then a few finely carved slices of that, with a bowl of cubed honeydew melon or some pickled peaches – there's no reason why English cooked ham should not make just as good a first course as the raw Parma or Bayonne ham.

As for pudding, unless you feel you absolutely have to have at least the traditional mince pies (those who only eat the Christmas pudding because of the brandy or rum butter will find it equally delicious with mince pies), most people will be grateful if you skip straight to the Christmas dessert fruits. Usually one is too full to appreciate the charms of Malaga raisins, Smyrna figs, almonds, glacé apricots and sugar-plums; or you could perhaps finish up with a big bowl of mixed fresh pineapple and sliced oranges.

 ## COOKING FOR A FAMILY

YEAR AFTER YEAR my Christmas cooking follows the same old routine. Most of it is done for the benefit of my sister's large family of young children. And I start off by soaking and baking a whole gammon or a piece of one, so that if necessary it can be cut into during the three or four days before Christmas. For women with children coming home for the holidays these days are usually the most hectic of all, and it makes more sense to have a big cold joint of some sort ready before they arrive than to keep all the food until Christmas Day.

Then there is the stuffing for the turkey to be mixed in advance and stored – mine is a comparatively easy one made from butter, bread crumbs, masses of parsley, eggs, and grated lemon peel; but even so, it takes a little time. And so does the paring and cutting up of orange peel for Cumberland sauce, and the slicing of oranges for fruit salad, both to be stored in the fridge; and possibly there will be a piece of dry-spiced beef to bake and cool – children appear to like this as much as the grown-ups do. The turkey I don't get into the house until Christmas Eve. Then I cook it at once, because we always eat ours cold (although the children have hot gravy and vegetables with theirs for lunch, and think they're having a hot meal, which they are, or at any rate as hot as it would be by the time a hot turkey is carved and the dishes passed round and the plates cooled).

Christmas puddings I haven't made for years, and last year we didn't even have a bought one. My sister said she was fed up with the whole performance of boiling the thing on Christmas morning and the turning of it out and the mess and all the rest of it, because the children didn't really like it and it was a waste. I applauded her realistic attitude but felt nervous about it, wondering if the children might demand their rights even if they didn't really want them. But their mother knew what she was talking about. She made a huge supply of chocolate ice cream mixture, froze it in the trays of her outsize refrigerator as she needed it, and the children never once even asked what had happened to the pudding. Another friend of mine, with fewer but older children, says they only ever ate the pudding for the brandy butter that goes with it, and any complaints on this score she has now settled by making, every year, instead of the pudding, one large, open, mincemeat pie and serving the brandy butter with that.

One detail that changes from year to year is the first course of the Christmas evening meal that we eat after the younger children have been put to bed. Usually I make a vast supply of some cheap and cheerful vegetable soup – such as the carrot purée for which the recipe is included here in the "Soups" chapter.

I don't say I'd go in for all this semi-traditional performance if I were simply going to have a few grown-up friends in for a Christmas meal – in fact I know I wouldn't. I'd have something very straightforward and un-rich like a handsome piece of plain roast fillet of beef followed by a very best pineapple or a pyramid of shining, whole, translucent caramelized oranges, and give people's eyes and stomachs a rest from all those birds – the sight of which has begun to make one feel slightly nauseated long before Christmas week.

But there it is. Most Englishwomen with families get caught up in some way or other with the frenzy of festive preparations, the children appear to enjoy it all, and once all this cooking is done, it is done, and for a few days there isn't much to worry about. Except getting it all eaten up before it goes stale.

CHRISTMAS PREPARATIONS

THERE WAS A TIME when, a week or so before Christmas, I used to set about making gigantic game and pork terrines and chicken liver pâtés, huge supplies of vegetable soups, jar after jar of Cumberland sauce, bowl upon bowl of fruit salad. Whether it was that the sight of so much food put people off, or that the Christmas festivities engender a tension that removes everybody's appetites, or simply that guests never materialized in quite the hordes one expected, I found that much of the food was regularly wasted.

What one comes to realize after years of organizing Christmas food supplies is that, the main celebration meal apart, there are always members of the family who tend to make their meal off snacks and bits and pieces. They just don't want to sit down to formal meals, and, while a varied supply of ready-cooked food is necessary to supplement the cold turkey or goose, pâtés and terrines are perhaps too rich and fat and vegetable soups too thick and filling.

Nowadays, my reserve stores consist of plainer and less demanding dishes such as cold tongue, a joint of cold spiced or salt beef and another of gammon from which everyone can carve a slice or two for themselves when they feel like it; there will also be plenty of fruit and salad stuffs of a kind that are both long-keeping and versatile – melons and oranges, Belgian endives and celery, hard, white cabbages and good carrots for making raw salads or hors-d'œuvre. For soups, there will inevitably be a quantity of stock made from the carcass of the Christmas bird (and it is a sound idea to make it swiftly rather than to wait until the creature has been hanging about in the larder for several days – and to enrich it with a piece of stewing beef bought especially for the purpose).

To take the place of the fat, pork-based pâtés and terrines, a beef loaf cooked rather in the same manner, but leaner, drier and easier on the digestion than liver and pork pâtés, makes an admirable stand-by, comparatively cheap, very easy to cook, and popular, or so I have found, with one and all.

Other Christmas Preparations

NOWADAYS IT IS difficult to realize that no Christmas preparations were made until the week before the day itself. All our excitement was packed into a short space. The boys were on holiday and all over the place. Mother was mostly in the kitchen, presiding over mincemeat and puddings. I was set to clean currants, squeeze lemons and cut up candied peel. Barnholt lent a hand at chopping the suet, but kept making raids on the lumps of sugar tucked away in the candied peel, which he assured me were very hard and nasty in the mincemeat, but had no ill effects on him.

M. VIVIAN HUGHES
A London Family 1870–1900
Oxford University Press, 1946

LIFE AFTER CHRISTMAS

ON THE ASSUMPTION that Christmas Day meals must take the traditional form, with all the preparation, last-minute basting, boiling, dishing up, carving and serving entailed, to say nothing of the exhaustion attendant upon the cooking of such food, most people are glad to plan the rest of the holiday entertaining with a view to reducing work, washing up, and strain. It should not be so difficult. There are meals that may be eaten at ease and enjoyed with the wines, the port, and the brandy, which are part of the grown-up enjoyment of Christmas.

One meal of roast turkey hot, one of roast turkey cold, are enough during three or four days – for a different turkey try the Bolognese way of cooking the breasts in butter, with ham and cheese; the rest of the bird will be excellent stewed in white wine (see the recipes included here). With the livers of turkey, chicken, duck or goose make a pâté (see the pâté recipes in "Cold Meats") a day or two before Christmas. Sealed with a layer of pork fat or butter and stored in the larder it will be a valuable aid to easy entertaining. Here are one or two suggestions for dishes entirely unconnected with Christmas fare. A luncheon, for example, consisting of some sort of pasta with a tunny fish or other unusual sauce, followed by a salad, cheese and fruit would provide a welcome rest for us all. A dish of scrambled eggs liberally sprinkled with grated Parmesan, followed by cold ham with a celery mayonnaise, would make another easily prepared luncheon. Green peas, a couple of chopped chicken livers and a handful of broken-up pasta cooked in good stock prepared from the carcass and giblets of chicken or turkey and served with grated Parmesan makes a soup for the evening meal both refreshing and comforting. As a change from Christmas pudding hot, cold, or fried, serve a water ice, the most refreshing possible sweet after rich and heavy food. Mincemeat well laced with rum or brandy makes a good filling for a sweet omelette.

✳ It's Older Than You Think ✳

Long before Christianity brought with it the celebration of Christmas, December was a time for feasting, rites and revellery. The Druids, as the British Farm Produce Council points out, made sacrifices at the time of the winter solstice, leaving as their legacy to us mistletoe, then a sacred plant, now an integral part of seasonal decorations.

The Romans had their Saturnalia — the festival of Saturn — enjoyed with much merry-making, official holidays, decorating of the houses with evergreens and the giving and receiving of presents.

Our Saxon forebears followed the Scandinavian custom of burning the Yule log. Centuries later, in Devonshire, the log was known as "ashton fagot." It was customary every time the log crackled in its burning to have a drink provided by the master of the house. This was usually cider or an "egg-hot," which was cider heated with eggs and spices.

There was a time when in the homes of the wealthy a succulent boar's head was the centerpiece of the Christmas spread. This was banned at the time of the Commonwealth (when it was believed that Christmas celebrations were pagan and should not be observed), much to the dismay of the tallow-chandlers who found it difficult to sell mustard, then a traditional accompaniment to the boar's head and to pork brawn.

The boar's head never returned to popularity but, luckily for us, other seasonal fare came back with a flourish, Christmas pies, for instance. There were coffin- or crib-shaped pies filled with a mixture of finely chopped meat, dried fruits, sugar and spices. They, too, were banned by the Puritans even though they had been popular since at least the times of the Crusaders.

The Puritans referred to them as "Superstitious pies, Christmas pies and also as minc'd pies". . . and over the ensuing years these pies became transformed to the mince pies we love today.

Plum-porridge also survived and was welcomed back at the time of the Restoration. This was a thick broth of meat, fruits and spices served at the start of the meal. It was the origin of our Christmas pudding.

Fashions in Christmas meats changed over the years. Gone were the lavishly decorated peacocks, sometimes gilded with gold paint, and in their place goose became a national favorite. This in turn gave way to turkey as the main attraction.

BRITISH FARM PRODUCE COUNCIL
December 1978

First Courses

Avocado

· II ·

AVOCADOS ARE so delicious and easy for a first course that sometimes I wonder why one bothers with anything else. There are, of course, several answers. They are fairly expensive. It is difficult to buy ripe ones when you need them. And even the finest things pall if you have them too often. But at Christmas time I feel it's really important to have a supply of anything which saves work and anxiety. So, at least ten days before Christmas I lay in a stock of very hard, unripe avocados. In a warm kitchen even very hard avocados will mature in ten to fifteen days.

Here I'd like to have my say about the detestable way avocados are so often treated. Filling them up with prawns or crab meat is just awful, a total wrecking of two good things at one blow. Is this ghastly custom simply a manifestation of conspicuous consumption, in the manner of people putting caviar inside rolls of smoked salmon? That one was certainly a brilliant idea for the sabotaging of two luxuries with no trouble at all.

I fully realize that I am unlikely to convert anyone already confirmed in their wicked ways, so will say no more here except that a fine ripe avocado with a little salt, lemon juice and perhaps a trickle of lightly fruity olive oil is to me one of the world's luxuries. And fancy dressings, Worcester sauce, sugar, ketchup, sticky corn oil or curry powder come not nigh my avocado pear.

✦ Egg Mayonnaise ✦

It may seem superfluous to give a recipe for so basic a dish as egg mayonnaise, but sometimes, in the search for originality, the most obvious dishes are forgotten. No one need ever be ashamed to offer their guests a well-made dish of egg mayonnaise, for it is always appreciated.

Having prepared a generous amount of really good thick mayonnaise according to the recipe given in "Sauces, Pickles and Chutneys," arrange it spoonful by spoonful on a flat oval or round dish. On top go the shelled hard-boiled eggs, cut in half lengthways and placed cut side down. Then the smallest possible sprinkling of very finely chopped parsley and absolutely nothing else whatever.

This is a filling dish, and three eggs for every two people should be more than enough.

✦ Egg Mayonnaise with Parsnip Cream ✦

This is a variation on the Cream of Parsnips with Ginger and Eggs in the "Vegetables" chapter. Make a parsnip purée as described in that recipe. Instead of the cooking water, stir in 2 or 3 tablespoons of thick jelly-like mayonnaise made with good olive oil and acidified with lemon juice instead of vinegar. Spread this purée on a flat dish. Arrange halved hard-boiled eggs on the top. Strew with parsley. A delicious little first course.

Cream Cheese Double cream cheese – not to be confused with the thin and sour concoction called cottage cheese – is a most versatile sweet or savory ingredient. With guava jelly or quince paste and wheat-meal biscuits, it is a cheese and dessert course in one. Gently heated, mixed with butter, grated Parmesan and roughly broken walnuts, it provides a beautiful sauce for pasta. With sugar and whisked egg whites folded in it makes a lovely sweet dish in the French manner. With bacon, fresh cream and egg yolks it becomes a delicate filling for a quiche. With honey, egg, spices and a short pastry flan case you can turn it into a most exquisite Greek island honey pie.

CREAM CHEESE CROÛTONS

A basic and useful recipe for almost any kind of soft white cheese.

Mash 4oz of soft curd, cream or milk cheese or demi-sel with 4 tablespoons of grated Cheddar, Gruyère, Parmesan, or any other hard cheese you have to hand. Add plenty of freshly milled black pepper and chopped fresh parsley or tarragon or a few chopped celery leaves. Then stir in one whole, well-beaten egg.

Spread this mixture on not-too-thick slices of white, brown, or French bread from which you have cut the crusts. There is enough for twelve croûtons. On top of each put little pieces of anchovy fillet and halved stoned black olives.

Put the croûtons on a baking sheet and cook them near the top of the oven for 15 minutes at 325°F.

Incidentally, this cream cheese mixture, made in quantity, spread on little fingers of bread and cooked in just the same way, is extremely good for a drinks party. The egg in the mixture makes it stay put instead of running all over the place as most cheese mixtures do.

⇥ A White Chicken Cream ⇤

This is a delicate dish based on a fine Italian budino di polio, *a kind of chicken mousseline for which the recipe was given to me twenty-five years ago by the proprietor of the then very famous Papagallo restaurant in Bologna. That delicious little chicken confection was cooked in tiny ramekins, turned out and served in a clear chicken broth. It was elegant food, and a lot of work. Pounding and sieving the chicken meat took so long that I made the dish only for very special occasions. Food choppers and processors have now changed all that, making it feasible to experiment often and with any amount of variations.*

It had dawned on me one day when studying early Italian recipes for biancomangiare, *French* blancmanger *and Spanish* manjar blanco, *that those spiced chicken and almond dishes of medieval Europe (they were certainly of Persian-Arab origin, and there were many variations) were in a sense the ancestors of my* budino di polio. *The almonds of the old recipes had been replaced with grated Parmesan, the ginger and sugar with nutmeg and salt, the bread thickening with eggs. For this recipe I have to a small extent reversed the process. To a small extent only, however — enough to make a change of flavor, provide a little surprise, without the slightest pretense that the end result is anything but a completely modern dish. Although perhaps not quite so modern as the dishes at those medieval feasts currently fashionable in manor house hotels and stately homes where the sole historical aspects of the meals are the names on the menu.*

You start off with a cold poached 4lb chicken cooked as described in the "Poultry and Game" chapter.

For two 1¾ pint moulds or loaf tins weigh out 1½lb of breast and wing meat freed of skin and bone. Other ingredients are 4oz of skinned almonds, 2 tablespoons of soft bread crumbs, salt and pepper, a small piece of fresh ginger, ½ pint of cream – single will do, or use half and half double cream and milk – or clear chicken broth, and 4 eggs. For decorating the creams when cooked and turned out: about 2oz of pine nuts.

Put all the chicken meat into the food chopper or processor. Reduce almost to a purée. Turn into a mixing bowl.

Separately, grind the skinned almonds and the soft bread crumbs. It is important to grind them very fine. Amalgamate them with the chicken. Season with salt and a little freshly milled pepper. Grate in about 1 teaspoon of ginger. Taste for seasoning, adding a little more ginger and salt if necessary. Stir in the cream, then the well-beaten eggs.

Have ready two lightly buttered loaf tins of 1¾-pint capacity, or one large round one (Teflon-lined tins make the ultimate turning-out of the creams much easier), a baking tin half filled with water, and two pieces of foil to cover the tins.

Fill the tins with the chicken mixture and fit on the foil. Cook the creams in the tin of water, on the shelf below center of a very moderate oven, 325°F, for approximately 50 minutes, or until the creams are just firm to the touch. Leave to cool before transferring them to the fridge.

To turn out the creams stand the tins in cold water for 5 minutes before inverting them on to flat oval dishes. From non-stick tins they should slip out easily. If they need assistance, remember to use a wooden or plastic spatula to help ease them out, otherwise the Teflon linings will be damaged.

To decorate the creams, put the pine nuts on an ovenproof plate in a moderate oven and let them toast for 10–15 minutes. Careful, though: they burn easily. Plant the top and sides with the little nuts, upright on the tops and projecting sideways at the corners and on the sides, like the spines of a hedgehog. It is very simple to do and the effect is charming and original.

Serve the creams like a pâté, as a first course, simply with a light lemony mayonnaise or Lemon and Celery Sauce as given in the "Sauces, Pickles and Chutney" chapter.

Note

An alternative to chicken would be, obviously, the cold turkey. I have also made many similar creams from fish, usually in half quantities and using leftover turbot, salmon, salmon trout or monkfish. I think that crab meat would be delicious treated in the same way. The four-teenth- and fifteenth-century Italian biancomangiare for fish days were made with eels, tench, pike and even lobster.

POTTED MEATS AND FISH

Mackerel

POTTED MEATS and fish pastes, these very English delicacies, make excellent first course dishes all the year round. During the Christmas season they are a real blessing. Easy to make, easy to store, easy to serve, certainly easy to eat, I never yet met anyone who didn't like them.

I first wrote about potted meats and fish in an article published in *Nova* magazine in April 1965. Three years later, having had enough of making copies of my article for people who had either lost the original or more often had heard about it but never seen it, I republished the piece, with two or three extra recipes, in a little booklet, *English Potted Meats and Fish Pastes.*

It did, I think, play some part in the revival of these characteristically English specialties. At any rate I've seen the recipes turning up in many other publications, the introductory notes too, and the passages I quoted from George Borrow's *Wild Wales* and Major Connolly's booklet whimsically called *Pottery by "a Potter."* So my initial work and modest research of 1965 have done a little good, and very glad I am to know it. But our modern kitchen machines have done more to popularize potted meat and fish than all the nation's cookery writers put together. Electric blenders were, of course, already in common use when I first started making potted tongue, smoked haddock paste and so on, and they did the job well enough. Later came food processors, which do a fine job of chopping and puréeing.

In 1984, I included the entire content of my 1968 booklet in the anthology *An Omelette and a Glass of Wine.* Here is one recipe that never made it in print before.

✦ Potted Smoked Mackerel ✦

The smoked mackerel fillets popular nowadays are admirable for this recipe. I find them more delicate than the whole smoked fish, as well as more economical. With mackerel, rich in fat, the minimum of extra butter is needed.

For 4 fillets or 1lb of mackerel allow 4oz of butter, the juice of one small lemon, seasonings of a very little salt and a few grains of cayenne. Optionally, a teaspoonful of fennel seeds or aniseed. Clarified butter for sealing.

Peel the skin from the fillets and pick out any little bones on the sides. Break up the fish, put it with the butter, lemon juice, and seasonings in the food processor or blender. Reduce all to a smooth paste. Taste for seasoning. Turn into a terrine or other dish of about 1-pint capacity, or two or three smaller ones. Smooth down the tops, cover with foil, refrigerate over-night. Next day remove the foil, seal with clarified butter. Serve chilled, with hot brown toast or thin slices of brown bread.

Note

Clarified butter is butter from which impurities and sediment have been removed. To prepare it, melt a large piece of unsalted butter over low heat and let it simmer for a few minutes until the surface is bubbling. Cool briefly, then pour through a sieve lined with damp muslin into a jar. Refrigerate when cold and use, melted, to cover potted fish and meat or for cooking. JN

⤳ PRAWN PASTE ⤶
An excellent little first course dish for three or four people.

½lb of peeled cooked prawns; 4–6 teaspoonfuls of olive oil; seasonings of cayenne pepper, dried basil, and the juice of a fresh lime or lemon. For a more spiced flavor add a saltspoon of crushed coriander or cumin seed.

Mash or pound the prawns to a paste – in a blender or food processor this can be done very quickly. Very gradually, add the olive oil. Season with cayenne pepper and about a ½ tea-spoon of dried basil warmed in the oven and finely crumbled. Add the strained juice of half a lemon or of a whole fresh lime (when available, the lime is much the better choice). When the mixture is smooth, and is seasoned to your satisfaction –

salt may or may not be necessary; that depends upon how much has already been cooked with the prawns – pack it into a little jar or terrine. Cover, and store in the refrigerator. Serve chilled, with hot thin toast. Do not attempt to store for more than a couple of days.

SMOKED COD'S ROE PASTE

Jars of smoked cod's roe can be bought these days from nearly any civilized grocer or fishmonger; it is food that makes a good-value, last-minute buy for the Christmas weekend and after. Made into a paste with oil and lemon, its sharp, clean, salty flavors come as a shock, a relief, and finally a stimulus after the soft plumminess of contemporary Christmas food.

A good method shown me long ago by Charles Bérot, chef-patron of the Escale Restaurant at Carry-le-Rouet near Marseilles, is to put the roe in a bowl with a little water (4 tablespoons for the contents of a 6oz jar) and leave it overnight. Next morning you pour off the excess liquid and the paste is then easily malleable and somewhat desalted as well, which does no harm. M. Bérot uses *botargue*, the compressed roe of a mullet that haunts inshore waters; it is an ancient product of the nearby lagoon fishing village of Martigues (the Sardinians have a similar product, so do the Greeks; the best of theirs comes from Missolonghi where the local name of this particular mullet is *baphes*; the roe, preserved in a casing of yellow wax, is known as *avgotaracho*), and is drier, much harder and saltier than smoked cod's roe. M. Bérot used to serve the paste as an hors-d'œuvre although the moment when it seemed to me at its best was at eleven o'clock one morning, with hot toast and cold white wine on the Escale's terrace, a shimmery view of the Mediterranean far below.

To make the paste, pound a very small piece of garlic, say half an average-sized clove; add to it the softened cod's roe and stir until it is quite smooth; gradually add, in alternating order, 4 tablespoons of olive oil, 2 tablespoons of water, the juice of half a lemon; finally, a sprinkling of cayenne. Some people add softened bread crumbs or a mashed potato, and call the compound *taramasalata*, which it does indeed very much resemble, except that, as I remember, in Greece the cooks add an almost overwhelming quantity of garlic and lemon, no doubt because *taramas*, their version of preserved cod's roe, packed in barrels, is very salty and dry. On its home ground Greek *taramasalata* is very different from the version served in all the London Cypriot restaurants.

✣ RILLETTES D'OIE ✣
Although it is not orthodox to make this dish with cooked meats,
a piece of roast goose mixed with uncooked fat pork makes
excellent rillettes and is a useful way of using up the Christmas
goose, for the rillettes can be stored for a few days until
this sort of food can once again be faced.

Suppose you have a leg of goose and perhaps a few good pieces of the carcass meat left, then buy 1½–2lb fresh belly of pork, and have the rind cut off. Remove the bones as well, and cut the meat and the goose roughly into 1 inch square pieces.

Put them into an oven pot, adding about 4 tablespoons of the fat saved when the goose was cooked. Pour in about ¼ pint of water, bury a bouquet of herbs and a crushed clove of garlic in the center of the meat, season with a teaspoon of salt and a little pepper. Cover the pot and cook in a very slow oven (275°F) for about 4 hours, until the meats are swimming in their own clear fat. Empty the whole contents of the pan into a sieve standing over a big bowl, and let the fat drip through. Slightly mash the meat, taste it for seasoning and add salt and pepper if necessary, then, with a fork in each hand, pull it into shreds. Pack these very lightly into glazed earthenware or china jars, leaving plenty of room for the fat. When this has cooled, pour it, leaving behind any sediment and juices, over the rillettes, completely filling the jars and covering the top. Put lids on the jars, or tie greaseproof paper over them. If they have to be stored in a refrigerator rather than a larder, take them out some hours before serving, for rillettes should be soft, rather like potted meat. Serve them as an hors-d'œuvre, with bread or toast, but butter will not be needed.

→ POTTED SPICED BEEF ←

With ½ lb of cooked spiced beef (see Spiced Beef for Christmas), including a good proportion of fat, and approximately 6oz of clarified butter (see the note with the recipe for Potted Smoked Mackerel), a most excellent potted meat can be made. No extra spices are needed.

Cut the beef, with its fat, into chunks; reduce them to a paste in the blender or food processor, adding 3oz of the clarified butter as chopping proceeds.

Pack the paste into a pot or pots (it will fill a ¾ pint dish), press it well down, smooth the top with a palette knife, chill thoroughly before warming the remaining clarified butter and pouring it over the top of the beef to form a complete seal.

Cover the pot or pots with foil and store in the refrigerator.

Potted meat should be eaten very cold with hot thin toast. Originally a breakfast dish, it makes a delicious first course for lunch.

[Additional recipes for first courses may be found in the "Cold Meats" chapter; see also the recipe for Chicken Livers with Rice in the "Poultry and Game" chapter, and Carottes Râpées and Céleri-rave Rémoulade in "Winter Salads."]

✳ Christmas in Rome ✳

The next day was Christmas Eve of the first Christmas of the war. Simon had said he'd be damned if he went home this year and serve them right. Of course, dear boy, Anna said, you must stay with us. She, in her eclectic way, had kept up with some and discarded other of her native customs. Christmas had never meant much to her. So during the years in Rome, she usually gave a large dinner-party for Thanksgiving but was content to go through Christmas as the Romans used to, doing a little eating and drinking, visiting the flowered festive churches. Her only personal contribution had been the fussless giving of some excellent presents. So Simon found himself spending the whole festival without a carol, a cracker or a suet pudding. On Christmas Eve the three of them with Mr. James sat down to a well-cooked dinner which ended with fresh fruit. Later on the ladies drove to midnight mass, and on their return there was very hot soupe à l'oignon gratinée and some vintage champagne. (Since it is always a pleasure to record such things: it was Krug 1904, and because of the onion soup it was Extra-Dry, not Brut, and there was as much of it as anyone might drink.) Simon learnt from an envelope that he had been given what amounted to a blank account at his booksellers. "I always think it's nicer to be able to choose oneself," said Anna.

"I do agree," said Simon in a loving voice.

December 25th and 26th were much like any other days except that, none of them wishing to venture out, they played some three-handed bridge. There was also a large Strasbourg pâté which Simon and Constanza ate up in one sitting, Anna was tactful and did not say a single hinting word. She was bustling and smiling in a way that reminded Constanza of her mother in the early days, and this new serenity struck fear into her heart. She would look at Simon, sunning himself in full favor, and could not forgive him. Simon felt he had never spent a more agreeable Christmas.

SYBILLE BEDFORD
A Favorite of the Gods
Collins, 1963

Soups

⇥ FISH CONSOMMÉ ⇤

For the first course of my Christmas dinner, there must be something hot and inspiring – a cup of what is to me quite the most marvelous and stimulating of soups ever created, a deep carnelian-clear and concentrated fish consommé, an essence of Mediterranean fish and shellfish made aromatic with leeks and tomatoes, fennel stalks, lemon peel, olive oil and white wine.

N<small>O COOKERY BOOK</small> that I know gives a recipe for this consommé. I have made it myself from time to time, but I have never written down the formula. My kitchen notebooks contain a number of entries regarding it: "used a turbot head and two John Dory carcasses" – "shells of a dozen Dublin Bay prawns" – "winter tomatoes no good, too acid, used tin of Italian peeled tomatoes, wonderful color" – "no white wine open, used vermouth instead, thought was better" – "two whites of egg for clarifying not enough. Had to do it again. Four to start with?" – "Some sort of lobster or prawn shell flavor essential" – "English crab meat too rich" – "pint of boiled prawns, shells and all. Wasteful.

It's the shells that provide the flavor" – "Stewed four chopped leeks, two carrots, four tomatoes in oil then added wine, fennel, garlic, saffron, sliced lemon, celery leaves. Then fish carcasses and heads; salt; six to eight pints water. Simmered one hour."

An organized and formal recipe still eludes me. This is partly because the soup is made in several stages; partly because every time the quantity and the kind of fish, the flavoring vegetables and aromatics vary; and again, somehow, whatever quantity of ingredients I start out with, in the end the consommé always seems to have reduced itself to enough for 4 cups and no more. The general principles are that you make a very strong vegetable and fish broth, a basic *soupe de poissons* or *brodo di pesce* of the kind common all along the shores of the Mediterranean, and having strained it, you chop up a pound or two of very ripe sweet squashy tomatoes, skins and all, and in a heavy wide deep pan, without oil or butter but with a little salt and sugar, you simmer these tomatoes down until they are quite thick and a rich wallflower orange color. Into the pan you then pour your saffron-yellow fish broth. When it has cooked with the tomatoes long enough to take some of their color and flavor, when it looks like molten bronze, then you strain your soup again (if you start on the clarification process now, with the tomatoes still in the soup, you will for certain have to do it all over again), and you put it back into the pan with the slightly frothed egg whites – allow two to 1 pint – and when the albumen, after 10 minutes or so of scarcely perceptible simmering, has done its clarifying work and formed a kind of crust to which are adhering all the impurities which were clouding the soup, leaving the broth underneath clear and limpid, then turn off the heat and leave the soup to cool for a while before straining it clear through a cheesecloth or four thicknesses of butter muslin placed in a large strainer or colander over a deep bowl or tureen.

When you heat up the beautiful consommé for serving, you may find it necessary to adjust the seasoning, to add a drop or two of brandy or Madeira, even of anisette or Pernod. To make cheese croûtons to serve with this Mediterranean essence, cut some thin slices of French bread. Rub them with a cut clove of garlic, bake them golden and dry in a low oven, sprinkle them thickly with grated Parmesan, return them to the oven until the cheese begins to melt.

⤙ POTATO, TOMATO AND CELERY SOUP ⤚

The outside sticks of 1 head of celery, 2 large leeks, 2 large potatoes, ½lb of tomatoes, 2oz of butter, 1¾ pints of water, salt, 2 teaspoons of sugar. To finish the soup, the yolks of 2 eggs and a little parsley or lemon thyme.

Cut the cleaned vegetables into dice and slice the tomatoes. Melt the celery and leeks in the heated butter. Do not let them brown. When they are transparent add the potatoes and the tomatoes. Cover the pot and cook extremely gently for 15 minutes. Add the water, a little salt, and the sugar. Cook for about half an hour. Sieve through a fine mesh sieve or a food mill.

To serve, beat the egg yolks in a bowl with a little of the soup. Heat up the soup. When it is very hot, lower the heat, stir in the egg mixture, and continue stirring until smooth and of the consistency of cream. Add the chopped herbs.

This is one of the most subtly flavored of all these vegetable soups, and it can, if the richness of the egg yolks seems too much, be served without this thickening, or with a little cheese stirred in instead. A good soup with which to start the Christmas dinner.

↦ Mushroom Cream Soup ↤

*There are hundreds of variations on mushroom cream soup. Here
is one which I find particularly successful. No stock is necessary.*

For four good helpings you need ½lb of mushrooms – preferably large open ones; ½oz of butter, 1 small clove of garlic,
seasonings of salt, coriander seed and nutmeg, a béchamel
sauce made with 1 tablespoon each of butter and flour and
approximately ½ pint of milk. For finishing the soup you
need another ½ pint of milk, about 2 tablespoons of dry white
vermouth, 2 or 3 tablespoons of chopped watercress, approximately ¼ pint of cream.

Rinse the mushrooms, wipe them with a soft cloth. Chop
them fairly finely. Put them in a saucepan with the butter.
Let them cook for a couple of minutes, until the juice runs.
Add the crushed garlic, salt to taste, half a dozen crushed
coriander seeds, a little nutmeg. Cover the saucepan and
leave the mushrooms to stew for 5 minutes.

In another saucepan make the béchamel sauce with the
butter, flour and warmed milk. Season it well, and let it cook
gently until it is quite smooth, and all trace of the taste of
flour has vanished. Stir the mushrooms into the sauce. Cook
for a minute or two. Rub the mixture through a fine sieve.
This is quite hard work. I think the result makes it worthwhile, but when in a hurry, give it a whizz at slow speed in
the electric blender and leave it at that.

Return the soup to the saucepan. Heat it up with the addi-
tional milk, previously heated. Taste for seasoning. Stir in
the vermouth and the chopped watercress. Add the cream,
just before the soup is served.

Notes

1. *The flavor of this soup should be warm and subtly spicy. Don't overdo the coriander. A light medium-sweet sherry can be substituted for the vermouth. The watercress is an interesting addition, giving a slight peppery taste to the soup.*

2. *The consistency of the soup should be that of pouring cream, no thicker. So if it has turned out too thick, add more hot milk, or a little chicken stock should you have it.*

❧ VARIATION ☙

This is a variation on the foregoing recipe. Ingredients are much the same but the method is different. No béchamel is required. Apart from the ½lb of mushrooms, the butter and seasonings and 1 pint of milk, you need 2 teaspoons of potato starch (*fécule*) instead of the ordinary flour. Other ingredients are as above.

Having cleaned, chopped and cooked the mushrooms in butter with the seasonings, mix the 2 teaspoons of potato starch with a cupful of cold milk. Stir the mixture into the warm mushrooms. Gradually add the rest of the milk, stirring all the time, until the soup thickens, then sieve or whirl it in the electric blender as for the first recipe. Return it to the rinsed-out saucepan, reheat with extra milk if necessary, a little cream, sherry or vermouth, and chopped parsley or watercress.

⤳ PUMPKIN AND CELERY SOUP ⤶

Cheap, easy, mild, but quite an original and distinguished soup. Don't make it more than a day in advance – pumpkin tends to sour rather quickly. Serve it before red meat and game roasts, hot or cold; ham, pork, grilled or fried chicken, or baked or grilled fish. Avoid melon, marrows and pale creamy sauces in the rest of the dishes.

1¼ pints of milk, 2lb of pumpkin, a stick of celery or the leaves of a whole small head, salt, 1 pint of mild stock or water, butter, lemon juice, parsley.

Bring the milk to the boil and let it cool a little. Peel the pumpkin and discard seeds and cottony center. Cut roughly into small pieces and put in a large saucepan with the celery cut into small pieces and a scant tablespoon of salt. Cover with the stock or water and the strained milk. Simmer for about 30 minutes until the pumpkin is tender. Sieve, or purée in the electric blender. Return to the pan and when reheating add, if the soup is too thick, a little more stock or milk; stir in a good lump of butter, a squeeze of lemon juice and some chopped parsley.

With the addition of about 4oz of pounded shrimps, potted shrimps, peeled prawns or even crab meat you can turn this homely pumpkin and celery mixture into quite a grand shell-fish soup. But it will then need a second sieving if you want it to be really smooth and creamy. There will be enough soup for six helpings.

✢ TOMATO CONSOMMÉ ✦
This is simple, cheap and delicate.

Ingredients are a small parsnip, cut into 4 pieces, 2 carrots, sliced, a clove of garlic, 2 sticks of celery, a generous sprig of fresh tarragon or approximately a teaspoon of good, dried tarragon leaves, a few saffron threads, one 14oz can of Italian or Spanish peeled tomatoes or 1½lb of very ripe and juicy fresh Mediterranean tomatoes, 1½ pints of water, seasonings of salt and sugar, 1 pint of chicken stock. For clarifying the consommé, 3 egg whites. For the final flavoring, 1 teaspoon of Madeira.

Put all the ingredients except the chicken stock, egg whites and Madeira into a capacious saucepan. If you are using fresh tomatoes – but don't bother unless it is the height of the season and you have really sweet and wonderfully ripe ones – chop them roughly, skins and all. Season only very moderately, say one teaspoon each of salt and sugar to start with. You can always add more later. Simmer in the open pan for about 40 minutes. Line a colander with a dampened doubled muslin cloth and strain the broth. Don't press the vegetables, just let the thin liquid run through.

Return the broth to the rinsed pan. Add the chicken stock. Bring to simmering point. Beat the egg whites for a couple of minutes. As soon as they start to froth pour them into the simmering broth. Cover the pan. Simmer very gently, until the whites have solidified and formed a crust, and are thoroughly cooked. By this time all the particles and impurities in the broth will have risen to the top and will be adhering to the crust. Leave to cool a little. Filter through a piece of dampened muslin placed in a colander, over a deep soup tureen or bowl. The consommé should be as clear as glass and a beautiful amber color.

When you heat the consommé for serving – and not before – add the teaspoon of Madeira, and a little more seasoning if necessary. Serve in big cups. There should be enough for five helpings.

Notes

1. An unorthodox, but uncommonly successful way of clarifying the consommé is to transfer the saucepan, covered, to a low oven as soon as you have added the egg whites. You can leave it for an hour or more. The first time I saw someone doing this – it was a Moroccan cook with whom I worked briefly in Marrakesh – I was aghast. And when I saw how well the system worked, amazed. It has to be remembered that unless your egg whites are cooked into a solid crust, your consommé will never be truly clear and clean. The oven method is a good way of achieving this aim without over-reduction of the consommé and attendant loss of its delicate flavors.

2. Alternatives to chicken stock are beef, veal or pork stock. Or for a fish broth, a concentrated fish fumet. A non-alternative, I'll repeat that, a non-alternative is a bouillon cube. Water is a preferable one.

3. Please don't be tempted to double the prescribed dose of Madeira. (You won't taste anything but the wine.) If you have no Madeira, use white vermouth, or manzanilla, or any decent sherry.

4. To serve with the consommé it is a good idea to have some little croûtons or slices of good bread, sprinkled with olive oil, spread with grated Gruyère or Parmesan and baked in the oven.

→ Pastenak and Cress Cream ←

This is a lovely soup, a welcome change from the routine watercress and potato soup. Pastenak is the medieval English word for parsnip, a corruption of the Latin pastinaca. In Italy, parsnips are still pastinache, a prettier name than parsnip, to me forever associated with a character created by the immortal Beachcomber.

Ingredients for the soup – a French one in origin – are 1lb of youthful parsnips (there should be 6; don't buy large horny old roots – they are both wasteful and disagreeable in flavor), 1 pint of thin clear chicken stock, salt, 1 level teaspoon of rice starch (*crème de riz*) or fine ground rice, or potato starch (*fécule*), or arrowroot, 1 little punnet of mustard and cress, 2–3fl oz of cream. To serve with the soup, a bowl of little croûtons fried in clarified butter.

Scrub the parsnips. With a small sharp knife or a potato parer prise out the hard little pieces of core from the crowns.

Put the parsnips in a saucepan with cold water just to cover. No salt at this stage. Boil them until they are soft – about 25 minutes. Remove them with a perforated spoon and leave them on a dish to cool. Keep the cooking water remaining in the saucepan. There will be about ½ pint, a valuable addition to the soup.

When the parsnips are cool enough to handle, the skins can be rubbed off, although personally I don't find this necessary. In the process of sieving, or puréeing in a blender or food processor, all skin will be smoothly incorporated. Advice often given to discard the central cores of parsnips is presumably intended to apply only to the above-mentioned ancient and horny roots, the cores being so woody that I doubt if even the sharp-bladed food processors of these days could chew them up. The cores of parsnips in their prime, however, are soft as bone marrow, and have a sweet flavor and buttery texture, which are important to this soup.

Having, then, sieved the parsnips through a stainless steel wire sieve or whirled them in a blender, turn the resulting purée into a clean saucepan, stir in the reserved cooking water and the stock, adding a seasoning of salt – 2 or 3 level teaspoons should be enough, but taste as you go.

Put the teaspoon of whichever starch you are using in a small bowl, ladle in a little of the warmed soup, stir to a smooth paste, return this to the saucepan and stir well until the starch has done its work of binding the vegetable matter and the liquid content to a smooth but slightly thickened cream.

When the soup is hot cut off the leafy tops of the cress with scissors, chop them small, stir them into the soup. Finally add the cream.

Have the croûtons already fried in clarified butter and drained on kitchen paper. Serve them separately in a warmed bowl. There will be enough soup for five big cups.

Notes

1. If the soup is made the day before you intend to eat it, it will thicken again on the second reheating, so have a little extra stock or milk ready to thin it down again. The soup shouldn't be thicker than pouring cream.

2. Watercress is an alternative to ordinary cress, but in this soup the latter is preferable.

3. Rice starch, crème de riz, is also labeled ground rice, although it is much finer than the slightly gritty product we used to know under that name. Rice starch and potato starch, fécule de pommes de terre in French, are both useful for binding soups and, occasionally, a custard or other sweet sauce. Both are used in very small quantities, so a packet lasts for years.

✦ Carrot Soup ✦

¾ lb of carrots; 1 shallot or half a small onion; 1 large potato; 1oz of butter; seasoning; 1 pint of turkey, chicken or vegetable stock, or water if no stock is available; parsley and chervil if possible.

Scrape the carrots, shred them on a coarse grater, put them together with the chopped shallot and the peeled and diced potato in a thick pan with the melted butter. Season with salt, pepper, a scrap of sugar. Cover the pan, and leave over a very low flame for about 15 minutes, until the carrots have almost melted to a purée. Pour over the stock, and simmer another 15 minutes. Sieve, return the purée to the pan, see that the seasoning is correct, and add a little chopped parsley and chervil. Enough for three.

Sometimes boiled rice is served separately with this soup, which makes it pretty substantial. Fried bread crumbs or small dice of fried potatoes are alternatives.

✇ VARIATION ✇
This is a slight variation of the above recipe, and made in a larger quantity.

Prepare 1lb of carrots, 4 medium-sized potatoes and 2 chopped shallots as for the previous soup, and stew them in 1¼ oz of butter in the same way. Add salt and 2 teaspoons of sugar. Add 2 pints of stock, or half stock and half water. Cook until the carrots and potatoes are quite soft and then sieve them or purée them in the blender. Do not make too smooth a purée; there should be perceptible little pieces of vegetable in the soup.

Return the soup to the saucepan, heat it up, and if it is too thick add more stock or water; taste for seasoning; stir in a good large lump of butter (its very buttery flavor is part of the charm of this soup) and some very, very finely chopped parsley. This will serve six people.

For both these soups it is, of course, important to have good-quality carrots, and both the taste and the color of the soup will depend on this, and will vary accordingly. Young carrots will give a clear bright orange color and a sweet flavor; later in the season the full-grown carrots will give a yellow soup and will probably need more sugar in the seasoning.

The consistency of the soup depends to a certain extent upon the quality of the potatoes, which makes it almost impossible to give an exact quantity for the stock.

↠ LENTIL SOUP ↞

This is an obvious enough way of making a soup with the stock from the Christmas birds; all the same, it remains one of the best and most comforting as well as one of the cheapest and easiest soups to make.

Ingredients for six good helpings are 2 small potatoes, a large onion, ½ lb of red or yellow lentils, a strip of rind from a ham or piece of gammon tied up with a bouquet of herbs, 3 pints of stock (or half stock and half water), olive oil, lemon juice and seasonings.

Slice the peeled potatoes and onion, put them in a saucepan with the lentils, ham rind, bouquet and a little salt. Cover with the stock, bring to the boil and simmer for 40 minutes. Extract the bouquet and ham rind. Sieve the rest. Return the purée to the saucepan, thin with more stock if necessary and, when hot, taste for seasoning and stir in 3 or 4 tablespoons of olive oil and a little lemon juice. These last two additions are an enormous improvement to the soup. In this country we don't make nearly enough use of olive oil as a seasoning.

In Middle Eastern cookery, soups made from dried vegetables, such as beans, peas and lentils, are nearly always enriched with olive oil. It takes the place of the fat which, in the form of butter or cream, is so often added to vegetable soups in French cookery.

✦ POTAGE SAINT HUBERT ✦
*A fine soup for the days after Christmas, to be followed by
the cold turkey or a terrine of game.*

1lb of brown lentils, 1 onion, 1 leek, thyme, a bay leaf, salt and pepper, 1 pheasant, 4fl oz of cream.

Cook the soaked lentils in salted water with the onion, the white of the leek, the thyme and bay leaf and seasoning.

Roast the pheasant (this may sound wasteful, but an old bird can be used, and at Christmas time we can surely be a little extravagant), and when it is cooked cut the meat off the bones, and keep aside the best fillets, which you cut into dice.

Chop the rest of the meat in a food processor or pound it in a mortar. Strain the lentils, discard the bay leaf, reserve the liquid. Add the lentils to the meat and purée the mixture in the blender or put it through a fine sieve into a saucepan.

Moisten it with the lentil stock, adding this until the soup is the right consistency. When it is quite hot add the cream and the diced pheasant.

Any cold game could be used for this soup, so could the remains of a roast goose. The amounts given will serve eight people.

↝ Barley Cream Soup and Barley Salad ↜

A dual-purpose recipe which produces a soothing, untaxing soup and an excellently original salad, all in one cooking operation, seems to provide an answer, and a sound one, to the question of how best to utilize the stock made from turkey or chicken carcasses.

Into about 4 pints of turkey stock put 4–6oz of pearl barley, and some flavoring vegetables such as carrots, an onion, celery and a halved grilled tomato or two (for color). Cook extremely slowly, in a covered pot, in the oven if you like, for at least 2 hours. Strain off the liquid and sieve a little of the barley and the carrots and celery into it – just enough to make a thin cream soup, to which, when you heat it up, you add a little fresh cream, lemon juice and a few drops of sherry or Madeira.

The rest of the barley cooked in the soup is strained off, turned into a bowl, and while still warm, seasoned with salt, pepper and nutmeg, dressed with 3 or 4 tablespoons of olive oil and one of lemon juice or tarragon vinegar. Into the salad mix a few cubes of green or yellow honeydew melon (in the summer use cucumber) and, if you like, a few orange segments.

The idea for this salad stems from a Boulestin recipe that, on a first reading, sounded freakish. Boiled barley and oranges. . . . Boulestin, however, is a writer in whose taste one has faith, no matter how odd his recipes may occasionally sound. He gives, in this instance, no quantities and no method. Last year I tried out the idea, cooking the barley as explained above. I served the salad with cold tongue and chicken. It was most delicate and attractive – better, I thought, than the well-known rice salad made on similar lines.

To Make Stock from a Poultry Carcass

When making stock from chicken or turkey carcasses upon which little meat is left, there are two points to be made. First, use them quickly, without waiting for them to get dried up and stale. Second, it is a mistake to cook them too long, or a strong and unpleasant flavor of bone will result (this is what makes pressure-cooked stocks so horrible) and the stock will be cloudy. Whenever possible it is a great improvement to add a small proportion of raw veal or beef when making such stocks, and to add onions, carrots, celery, herbs.

✳ Christmas at Sea ✳

Christmas Day started at 11 in the morning with a bottle of champagne to cure the hangover. Round-the-Empire broadcast and the King's rather lugubrious speech at lunch. Dinner with a huge menu. Hors d'œuvre, soup, fried whiting, tinned asparagus, roast turkey and chipolatas, plum pudding, grapefruit ice. It was like peace. Toasts to the King, Churchill, Roosevelt (for W.), Sikorski (for the Pole), etc. Then the captain, mate and the chief came to the smoking-room. A shy R.N.V.R. officer tried to play hymns (the only tunes he knew), but the atmosphere by that time was not propitious. Played Sing, Say or Pay. Broke up traditionally at midnight with Auld Lang Syne, and afterward I settled down to chess with the Pole. One was less homesick than one had expected. Presumably that was the drink. Woke up at about 5 in the morning with an explosion; I thought that one of the convoy had caught it, but it must have been the clap of the wind as we changed course.

From the author's diary of a convoy
to West Africa, December 1941,
GRAHAM GREENE
In Search of a Character
The Bodley Head, 1961

Cold Meats

· IV ·

✣ TURKEY OR CHICKEN SALAD ✦

*The important point to remember about cold roast turkey is that
a tendency to dryness has to be counteracted. A mayonnaise would
seem to be the obvious answer, but in fact it is not in the least what
one wants to eat so soon after all the heavy Christmas food. On the
other hand, a salad made from a turkey and a vinaigrette dressing,
augmented with hard-boiled eggs, appears to be altogether a more
acceptable proposition. The ingredients may be precisely the same
as those for a mayonnaise, but the effect is quite different.*

FOR ABOUT ¾lb of cold turkey or chicken, freed of skin
and bone and sliced into thin, even pieces, make the
following sauce: chop 2 shallots with the well-rinsed
leaves of a bunch (about 1oz) of parsley and any other herbs
you may happen to have, such as tarragon and a little lemon
thyme; stir in a seasoning of salt and freshly milled pepper,
2 scant teaspoons of French mustard, 6 tablespoons of olive
oil and the juice of a small lemon.

Beat all the ingredients well together and then mix the
sauce with the pieces of turkey. Leave the whole mixture in

a covered bowl until serving time. Then arrange the salad in a shallow dish with sliced hard-boiled egg all round and, should they be available, a few peeled prawns, seasoned with oil and lemon, on the top. They make an excellent combination with turkey and chicken. Such things as capers, pickled cucumber, strips of crisp raw celery or cubes of melon can also be added to the salad.

✣ Bœuf en Salade ✣

To use a piece of cold spiced beef, or Bœuf à la Mode, *or beef from an* estouffat (*such as the* Estouffat de Bœuf Albigeois *given in the "Meats" chapter*).

At the bottom of a salad bowl put a layer of sliced tomatoes, seasoning them with salt and pepper, then a layer of small slices of beef, then a layer of cooked potatoes, also seasoned with salt and pepper. Pour over a vinaigrette dressing (oil, tarragon or wine vinegar, French mustard, a little sugar, capers, chopped chives, parsley and lemon peel). Garnish the salad with quarters of hard-boiled egg.

✣ Chicken Liver Pâté ✣

Clean ½–1lb of chicken livers carefully and remove any parts that look greenish, as they will give a bitter taste to the pâté. Melt 1oz of butter in a frying-pan; put in the livers, whole, and let them cook gently for not more than 5 minutes. They must remain pink inside. Take them from the pan and put them in a marble mortar. To the butter in the pan add 2 tablespoons of brandy and let it bubble; then 2 tablespoons of port or Madeira and cook another minute.

Add half a clove of garlic, salt and ground black pepper, and a small pinch of thyme to the livers and pound them to a paste. Pour in the butter mixture from the pan and 2oz of fresh butter. When all is thoroughly amalgamated and reduced to paste put it into an earthenware terrine in which it will come to within ½ inch of the top.

In a clean pan melt some pure pork, duck or goose fat (or butter); pour it through a strainer on to the pâté. There should be enough to form a covering about ¼ inch thick, so that the pâté is completely sealed. When the fat has set, cover with a piece of foil and the lid of the terrine, and store in the larder or refrigerator. It should not be eaten until two or three days after it has been made and as long as it is airtight will keep a week or two in the larder in cold weather, and several weeks in the refrigerator.

It is a very rich pâté and butter is not necessary with it. ½lb of chicken livers makes enough pâté for four or five people.

Note
The pâté can also be made in a food processor. JN

✦ TERRINE OF PORK AND DUCK ✦
For Christmas and holiday entertaining here is a recipe for a game pâté on a large scale, enough for 20–30 people according to how many other dishes there are to be. It is a rather firm pâté, easily sliced through for serving. It is all the better for being made three or four days in advance.

Quantities are 2lb each of belly pork and leg of veal, 1 wild duck (mallard), ½lb of back pork fat. For the seasoning you need 8–10 juniper berries, 1 large clove of garlic, 10 peppercorns, 2 teaspoons of salt, 2 small glasses of dry white wine, 3 tablespoons of stock made from the duck carcass with a little extra white wine or Madeira.

Remove rind and bones from the pork and mince it

together with the veal, or to save time get the butcher to do this for you. Partly roast the duck in order to facilitate the removal of all the flesh from the bones; chop this fairly small and mix with the pork and veal. Add 5oz of the fat cut into little pieces, the juniper berries, garlic and peppercorns all crushed together with the salt. Pour in the white wine, amalgamate thoroughly and leave in a cold place while you simmer the broken-up duck carcass and the trimmings for 20 minutes in a little water and wine, with seasonings, to make the stock. Strain it, reduce to 3 tablespoons, and add to the mixture (if it is necessary to expedite matters this part of the preparation can be dispensed with altogether; it is to add a little extra game flavor to the pâté).

Turn into a 3-pint terrine; cover the top with a criss-cross pattern of the rest of the pork fat cut into little strips. Cover with foil. Stand in a baking tin containing water, and cook in a low oven, 325°F, for 2 hours. During the last 15 minutes remove the foil, and the top of the pâté will cook to a beautiful golden brown.

One wild duck sounds a very small proportion for a game pâté, but it gives sufficient game taste for most people. If you like a more pronounced flavor, substitute a second duck for half of the veal.

✢ PORK AND CHICKEN LIVER PÂTÉ ✢

1lb each of belly pork and offcuts from leg of veal (usually sold as pie veal); ½lb of chicken livers; ½lb of back pork fat in one piece (if sold with the rind allow a little extra); 10–12 whole black peppercorns; 2 level dessertspoons of salt; a small piece of garlic; 2 tablespoons each of Cognac and white wine, Madeira, port or dry vermouth; a couple of bay leaves.

Mince or chop the pork, veal, ¼lb each of the cleaned chicken livers and the pork fat (minus rind). Use an electric chopper if you have one, rather than a mincer, and don't make the mixture too fine or smooth.

Turn all into a large mixing bowl. Make the seasoning mixture by crushing the peppercorns rather coarsely with the salt and the garlic (in a pâté a very small amount of garlic goes a very long way – be careful not to overdo it). Stir the seasoning into the meat, adding a tablespoon each of the brandy and wine, amalgamating it very thoroughly into the whole mass. You can work it with your hands, almost like bread dough. Leave the mixture for an hour or two, or overnight if it is convenient. Keep it covered.

Put the rest of the cleaned chicken livers into a small bowl with the rest of the brandy and wine, and leave to marinate until you are ready to make the pâté.

For cooking it you need a glazed earthenware or other terrine, no matter whether rectangular, oval or round and no matter whether with or without lid. What is important is the capacity, which should be from 1¾ to 2 pints. This sounds rather small for the quantity, but is correct. Alternatively two smaller ones can be used.

Have ready also the remaining de-rinded pork fat, sliced into narrow strips which will fit across the top of the terrine. Slicing the fat will be easier if it has been well chilled.

Pack a layer of meat into the terrine – enough to fill it by half – then a layer of the whole chicken livers, then a top layer of meat which should be domed up well above the rim of the container. There is a certain amount of shrinkage during cooking, and if the terrine is not packed full to start with, you will end up with a rather sad and shrunken-looking pâté. Hence the apparently small capacity of the terrine.

Put the 2 bay leaves on the top of the meat, and over them arrange the strips of fat, in a trellis pattern. Cover with a piece of foil, put the terrine in a baking tin half filled with water, cook low down in a moderate oven, 325°F, for 1¼–1½ hours. During the final half hour the foil can be removed to allow for the top of the pâté to brown. Take care though that it does not dry out. The pâté should still be pink and moist when it is cut, so when it has slightly shrunk from the sides of the terrine it is time to take it from the oven.

Leave the pâté to cool until the fat begins to set. Cover it with fresh foil and store in the refrigerator. Like most pâtés this one is at its best two or three days after it has been cooked. Serve it from its terrine, not turned out. Duck livers can be used instead of chicken livers, or the two can be mixed.

⇢ Pork and Veal Loaf ⇠

This is an especially useful dish at Christmas, when extra guests may turn up, and for picnics or buffet suppers. Serve it either as a first course, with toast or French bread, or as a main course with a salad and perhaps jacket potatoes.

For a large terrine (2½ pint capacity) you need the following ingredients and quantities: 1½lb each of minced uncooked fat pork and lean veal (choose belly of pork weighed without rind or bone, and the small veal trimmings from the leg cuts that butchers sell as pie veal; some butchers sell ready-minced veal and pork which is adequate, but don't buy sausage meat), and 4oz of bacon in the piece (a cheap cut will do very well) plus 3 or 4 rashers for the top of the loaf. Seasonings are 1 teaspoon of whole peppercorns, 2 teaspoons (approximately) of salt, 4 tablespoons of sherry or light port.

Put the two minced meats, and the bacon cut into small

cubes (minus rinds), into a big china or glazed stoneware mixing bowl. Crush the peppercorns together with the salt and stir them into the meat. Add the sherry or port and mix very thoroughly. If possible, leave, covered, for a couple of hours, so that the seasonings and wine have a chance to blend with the meat.

Now turn the whole mixture into your terrine. Because the meat in this type of dish shrinks quite a bit during the cooking it is essential that, initially, the terrine be packed absolutely full to the brim, the loaf slightly domed in the center.

Cut the bacon rashers into fine strips; arrange them in a lattice pattern across the top of the meat. Put on the lid.

Preheat the oven to 325°F. If you use an earthenware terrine, stand it in the oven in a tin of water; a heavy cast-iron terrine can be placed directly on the bottom shelf. Cook for one hour. Remove the lid, and leave for another 30 minutes.

Remove the terrine from the oven, leave to cool and set. Store in the refrigerator. The seasonings can, of course, be varied, a crushed clove or two of garlic can be added, 2 tablespoons of brandy or whisky substituted for an equal proportion of the sherry, a teaspoon of mixed powdered spices or crushed juniper berries added.

✦ SPICED BEEF LOAF ✦

Ingredients are 3½ lb of fairly finely minced beef bought from a reliable butcher, 4oz of fat mild bacon, 1 teaspoon each of dried basil and ground allspice, 2 heaped teaspoons of salt, 1 dozen peppercorns, 1 very small clove of garlic, 4 tablespoons of port, sherry or red wine, 1 tablespoon of wine vinegar.

Put the beef into a big china bowl, add the roughly chopped bacon, all the seasonings crushed together, the wine, and the vinegar. Mix very thoroughly, and if possible leave for a couple of hours so that all the flavors have a chance to penetrate the meat.

Turn the whole mixture into a 2½–3 pint loaf tin, or two smaller tins. The mixture will shrink during the cooking, so that, initially, the containers should be packed full to the brim. Stand the tins in a shallow baking tin filled with water and cook uncovered in the center of a slow oven, 325°F, for 1½ hours.

If the top of the loaf looks like getting too brown, cover with buttered foil or greaseproof paper.

Leave to cool, then store in the refrigerator or a cool larder.

To turn the loaf out of its tin simply run a knife round the edges and ease the loaf out on to a dish. Carve it in rather thin slices, and serve with a salad and/or sweet-sour pickled fruits, mild fruit chutney, or a mustardy sauce.

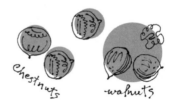

❋ A Country Christmas ❋

There was the smell of hot toast and ale from the kitchen, at the break-fast hour; the favorite anthem, the green boughs, and the short ser-mon, gave the appropriate festal character to the church-going; and aunt and uncle Moss, with all their seven children were looking like so many reflectors of the bright parlour fire, when the church-goers came back, stamping the snow from their feet. The plum-pudding was of the same handsome roundness as ever, and came in with the symbolic blue flames around it, as if it had been heroically snatched from the nether fires into which it had been thrown by dispeptic puritans; the dessert was as splendid as ever, with its golden oranges, brown nuts, and the chrystalline light and dark of apple jelly and damson cheese: in all these things Christmas was as it had always been since Tom could remember; it was only distinguished, if by anything, by superior sliding and snowballs.

GEORGE ELIOT
The Mill on the Floss, 1860

Poultry and Game

WHAT TO DO WITH THE BIRD?

A NICE THOUGHT, although perhaps an unworthy one, that when Christmas morning dawns, for four whole days there won't be any shopping to do. Or anyway no serious food buying. That means that for once the house won't be crammed with a lot of unnecessary food. And the surprising thing is that it is unlikely we'll be in any great danger of starving.

I suppose the question of what to cook with the bits of leftover turkey (good as it is cold, there does come a moment when it can't be faced again) or goose, ham and the rest will have to be pretty well planned beforehand, but this isn't really such a burden as everybody makes out. I don't believe, myself, in opening a whole lot of jars and bottles and tins to help out with the remains. I don't want a whole stack more oddments becoming problems in their turn. And on the whole, dishes made from already cooked birds and meat are very much more attractive if you treat them as if they were dishes in their own right. They only become squalid little horrors when you doll them up with a lot of ingredients without point or purpose.

So the only extra supplies I shall bother about are a few more eggs than usual, some cream in the refrigerator, the usual things like onions and carrots for soup stock, rice, a small supply of Parmesan or Gruyère cheese for grating, plenty of olive oil, lemons, and coffee, and a piece of pork to help out with a goose dish when the time comes. I suppose I might think about getting a tin of tunny fish or prawns to use in a salad, and perhaps a couple of refreshing honeydew melons from which either salads or dessert dishes can be made.

And if any of those marauding bands of persons who apparently roam the countryside calling themselves unexpected guests appear at my door – well, they'll have to make do with soup and an omelette and a glass of wine to help them on their way to their next victims. I think I'd feel less nervous anyway offering them this sort of food than I would if I'd made a lot of little surprises with names like Pantry Shelf Fishbits and Fantastic Belgian Meat Balls and Festa Turkey-Nut Logs. I didn't make them up, I swear I didn't. I read about them in a desperately sad American cookery book all about leftovers.

TURKEY AND STUFFINGS

Boulestin's Christmas Turkey The sanest words ever written about the Christmas turkey come from a Frenchman, Marcel Boulestin. "Take a turkey about nine or ten pounds in weight. There is no point in having a larger bird unless you are particularly fond of cold turkey. As it is, the one chosen will do once hot, once cold, once for rissoles, and the bones, etc., will be the making of a perfectly good soup."

To that serious advice so lightly given I can add only a plea that the "rissoles" – by which Boulestin didn't mean quite what is usually understood by the term – and the "perfectly good soup" be as swiftly made and consumed as is compatible with post-Christmas fatigue and surfeit.

✢ TURKEY WITH HERB AND BUTTER STUFFING ✢

For the stuffing for a 10–12lb turkey, mix ½lb of very fine bread crumbs (made from bread dried, but not colored, in the oven), the grated rind of 2 large lemons, the juice of 1, 6–8 tablespoons (1½–2oz, without stalks) of finely chopped parsley, with a little thyme, lemon thyme and marjoram if available, a very little salt, freshly milled pepper, ½lb of unsalted butter and 3 whole, well-beaten eggs.

Taste the mixture when it is all evenly blended; at this stage the lemon flavor should be quite pronounced, for it will lessen in the cooking; and, above all, poultry stuffing should not emerge tasting predominantly of bread.

The mixture can be made 2 or 3 days in advance, but do not take it frozen stiff from the refrigerator and put it straight into the bird, for the heat takes a long time to penetrate and if over-chilled the butter in the stuffing does not then start its work of lubricating the bird from the early stages of cooking.

Having stuffed the bird (crop and body), rub it very lavishly with softened butter, putting the lumps between the thighs and body; there can hardly be too much. Wrap it in equally lavishly buttered foil, put the bird on its side on a rack standing in a tin, and in the tin put a cupful or so of water. Have the oven preheated to very moderate, 325°F. A bird of this size takes 2¾–3½ hours to cook; at half-time it should be turned over, and 30 minutes before it is to be served take away the paper and turn the bird breast upward in the oven, so that it acquires a fine golden-brown surface. Even with all these precautions, one usually finds the legs a little under-cooked, but I don't think this matters much because they can all the better be used next day for a reheated dish.

The buttery juices in the pan are to be poured off into a small saucepan, a little glass of white wine or vermouth added, and the whole given a quick turn over the fire. For extra gravy, the giblets will already the previous day have been simmered gently with vegetables, herbs and, for my taste, a small piece – say ½–¾lb – of beef or veal to give extra flavor, for the taste of the stock produced by turkey giblets is rather insipid.

One more word about cooking the turkey. Do not try to cook a bird that practically fills your oven at a temperature very much higher than the one I have given. This is a point where one may very well be led astray by the temperature and timing given by professional chefs, for they are, probably, cooking in very large ovens in which there is plenty of room for air to circulate all round the object cooking. In small domestic ovens, all that happens if you attempt to cook your turkey in a hurry at high heat is that the outside of the bird is scorched long before the heat has penetrated the interior. And make sure that your turkey is still not half-frozen from the refrigerator when you put it in the oven.

The herb and butter stuffing is delicious for a roast capon or chicken. For a large bird, about 5–6lb, allow half quanti-ties. If any is left over, use it for stuffing tomatoes to be baked and served with the chicken.

A capon can be cooked in the same way, allowing approx-imately 2 hours' cooking time.

→ TURKEY STUFFED WITH CHESTNUTS AND APPLES ←
French cooks nearly always add pork or sausage meat (see next recipe) to the chestnut stuffing for turkey. It helps lubricate the

bird, and improves the flat taste of chestnuts. In this northern French recipe apples are also added. (The recipe is very similar to that for "Goose with Chestnuts and Apples." JN)

For an average turkey of about 12lb the proportions are 2lb of chestnuts, ½ pint of milk, 6oz of salt or fresh belly pork, 1lb of sweet apples, 2 shallots, parsley, an egg.

Make a crosswise incision across the rounded part of the chestnuts and roast them for 10–15 minutes in a moderate oven. Take out a few at a time and shell and skin them while still hot. Stew them in the milk, to which is added ¼ pint of water, until they are soft. This will take about half an hour.

Cut the pork into small dice, and cook for 10 minutes in a little water.

Peel and core the apples, stew them in a very little water until reduced to a purée. Mix with the pork and the drained and roughly broken up chestnuts. Season with salt and pepper and the finely chopped shallots and parsley, and bind with a beaten egg.

The stuffed turkey, liberally rubbed with butter, is roasted (on its side if possible) in a slow oven, covered with buttered paper or aluminum foil.

For a turkey of this size cooked at 325°F, the cooking time is about 3½ hours. Turn it over at half-time. Do not attempt to cook a large turkey in a small oven at a high temperature, for it will dry up and the outside will burn.

For the sauce, a little white wine can be added to the buttery juices in the pan, and the whole quickly boiled up in a small saucepan.

Note

Vacuum-packed chestnuts need no pre-cooking and can be broken up immediately. JN

✣ French Sausage Meat ✣

When a French recipe calls for chair à saucisses *— perhaps for the stuffing for a chicken or turkey, for paupiettes, stuffed tomatoes and so on — this simply means a pure pork mixture to be bought from the butcher or the charcutier. It will be made approximately in the proportions of twice the quantity of fat meat to lean and with the minimum of seasoning; no bread, of course, and no herbs; no preservatives or additives. This basic ingredient of French cookery is not normally obtainable at English butchers, for what we understand by sausage meat is a different affair altogether, and pretty stodgy it is when used for poultry or any other kind of stuffing.*

A friendly butcher will, however, mince the required amount of pork for you. The cuts to ask for are belly for the fat meat, and a piece of the upper part of the neck (scrag) or shoulder (sparerib) for the lean. Have it minced rather coarsely, minus the rind, of course, and yourself add the following seasonings: for 1½lb of sausage meat (i.e., 1lb of belly and ½lb of shoulder or neck), 1 teaspoon of coarse salt, 8 black peppercorns and, optionally, ½ teaspoon of ground allspice.

Crush the salt and peppercorns together, mix in the spice and blend thoroughly with the sausage meat.

With the addition of a beaten egg and chopped parsley this mixture can be made into delicious little croquettes or *boulettes de viande* to be fried.

→ RICE AND ALMOND STUFFING FOR TURKEY ←

For a 5–7lb turkey this delicately flavored rice stuffing is worth trying. I make it in a rather larger quantity than is actually needed for the bird, using the remainder next day for baked stuffed tomatoes (see the recipe for "Roast Capon") to serve as a hot first course before whatever may remain of the cold turkey. The mixture also makes an excellent stuffing for partridges – one heaped tablespoon for each.

Ingredients are 1 teacup of risotto rice, 2oz of sultanas, a bunch of parsley weighing approximately ½oz, a piece of onion weighing 1oz, a 2 inch strip of lemon peel, 2oz of shelled but unskinned almonds, the liver of the turkey, 2oz of butter, the juice of half a lemon, 1 teaspoon of salt, freshly milled pepper.

Cook the rice for 15 minutes in plenty of boiling lightly salted water. Put the sultanas in a cup of warm water. Chop the parsley, onion and lemon peel, and separately, and not too finely, the almonds. Cook the liver for a few seconds in a teaspoon of the butter, then chop it.

Mix the well-drained rice and sultanas with the other ingredients, add the lemon juice and seasonings, and finally the just-melted butter.

Because this mixture is not bound with an egg, the rice emerges flaky, light and dry, even after the fairly lengthy and slow cooking of the turkey, so that when the bird is carved the stuffing can be scooped out of the body and served separately, in a warmed dish.

→ ITALIAN STUFFING FOR TURKEY ←

3 prunes, half-cooked, and stoned; ¼lb sausage meat (see above); 3 tablespoons of chestnut purée; 2 small slices of bacon;

a small cooked pear; the liver and gizzard of the turkey; seasoning; butter.

Chop the ingredients finely and mix them all except the liver and gizzard. Add these when you have lightly sautéed the first mixture in a good lump of butter.

✣ PORK AND CHESTNUT STUFFING ✣

For a 12lb bird, ingredients are 1lb of chestnuts, milk, 1 small onion, butter, 1lb of minced fresh pork, a stick of celery, salt and pepper, 4fl oz of port or Marsala, 2oz of dried home-made bread crumbs, and 2 eggs.

Prepare the chestnuts as described for the stuffing with chestnuts and apples, put them into a saucepan and cover with half water and half milk. Simmer them very gently, covered, for about an hour, until they are quite soft but not mushy. (*See previous note on vacuum-packed chestnuts. JN*)

Meanwhile, in a large heavy pan, melt the chopped onion in a little butter. Put in the minced meat. Let it brown gently. Add the celery, cut in little pieces, and season with salt and freshly ground black pepper. Pour in the wine. Let it bubble a minute.

Cover the pan and simmer 10 minutes. Add the chestnuts, strained and broken up with a fork (for a stuffing I prefer not to purée them). Then, off the heat, stir in the bread crumbs and the beaten eggs. Do not worry if the mixture seems a bit liquid at this stage: by the time the bird is cooked it will have attained the correct consistency.

If minced pork is hard to find and you don't possess an efficient mincer, chops or belly pork can be cooked in the piece with the onion and then cut off the bone and chopped. Allow 4oz extra for meat on the bone.

⇢ Pork and Mushroom Stuffing ⇠

To 6oz of pork mince the other ingredients are ¼lb of mushrooms, 1oz of butter or pure pork lard, salt, 1 tablespoon of white wine, brandy or Madeira, a tablespoon of chopped parsley, 1 whole egg.

Wash and drain the mushrooms, chop them roughly. Heat the butter or pork lard in a frying-pan, cook the mushrooms in it for a minute, add a pinch of salt, then the pork mince. After another minute add the wine or brandy, the parsley and the well-beaten egg. A few more seconds and the stuffing is ready.

A mixture of this kind adds flavor and moisture to modern roasting chickens (there should be ample for a 4–5lb bird) and also – in half quantities – to guinea fowl and pheasant, but the seasonings can be varied in many ways. Lemon thyme or a little grated lemon peel can be included, lemon juice can be added instead of wine, the mixture can be stiffened with a couple of tablespoons of bread crumbs or, in the Italian manner, nutmeg and a tablespoon or two of grated Parmesan can go into the seasoning. And as a variation, about 4 tablespoons of chopped raw celery can replace the mushrooms.

❧ GIBLET GRAVY ❧

The giblet gravy of a turkey is best started off a day ahead of time. Put the giblets (keep the liver for another dish) with 2 carrots, 1 onion, a small glass of white wine or vermouth, a bouquet of herbs, ½lb of stewing veal, and 2 halved and grilled tomatoes into a small soup pot. Set over a low flame without other liquid. Let the wine cook and all the ingredients take color before adding salt and enough water to cover. Transfer the pot, covered, to a very low oven (perhaps at the same time as the bread for the stuffing is drying) for about 2 hours. Return it to the oven again, if there is room, while the turkey is cooking. At about the same time as you open the oven to take the foil off the turkey, remove the giblet stock, strain it, transfer it to a saucepan and keep it ready on the top of the stove for the final heating up.

❧ BONED TURKEY, STUFFED WITH TONGUE ❧
AND FORCEMEAT

Very clear instructions for this Victorian dish are to be found in a little-known and uncommonly well-thought-out book called *Cre-Fydd's Family Fare or Young Housekeeper's Daily Assistant*, published in 1864. Whoever Cre-Fydd was – and I have been unable to find anything about her – she makes most of her contemporaries, including Mrs. Beeton, look vague and disorganized.

I have tried Cre-Fydd's recipe, getting an 8lb turkey boned by my poulterers (I waited until after Christmas, when, the festive season having died down, turkeys are cheaper and I myself more disposed to face trying a new recipe). The result was very good, and decorative; but whereas Cre-Fydd recommends a celery sauce enriched with cream and egg yolks to be poured over the hot bird, I served mine cold, without sauce, and accompanied by a barley salad as described in the recipe for Barley Cream Soup. (Should you want to try the sauce, the recipe is included in the "Sauces, Pickles and Chutney" chapter.)

A boned turkey stuffed with a whole small cooked ox-tongue is a Victorian dish that I have always thought sounded attractive and sensible. Tongue and turkey meat make good foils one for the other. As centerpieces for the Christmas cold table both figure often enough as separate dishes. Together they must make a most decorative and delicious combination, especially good cold, I would think.

Here are Cre-Fydd's instructions: "Boil a small pickled tongue slowly for three hours; skin it and trim off the root, leaving only a portion of the fat. Make a stuffing as in the preceding recipe, send them both to the poulterer to be put into the turkey. Then follow the preceding recipe in all things."

The recipe that the reader is to follow "in all things" is for a boiled turkey with celery sauce, and the stuffing that the author refers to is as follows: chop ½lb of beef suet, rub 2oz of bread into fine crumbs, chop enough fresh parsley to fill a tablespoon; mix these together and season with a saltspoonful of salt, half a saltspoonful of white pepper, the eighth part of a nutmeg, grated, the grated rind of half a lemon, and the strained juice; half a saltspoonful of mixed sweet herbs, half a saltspoonful of thyme; add 2 well-beaten fresh eggs and 2 tablespoonfuls of cream.

For cooking the turkey, excellent and detailed instructions are given.

Put the stuffing into the breast of the turkey, fasten the skin loosely over it with skewers; rub the turkey with a cut lemon; cover the breast with thin slices of fat bacon; tie it in a clean white cloth; put it into an iron pot with sufficient water to cover it; boil it up quickly, then simmer gently till done.

A poult requires an hour and a quarter from time of boiling up; a turkey weighing ten pounds, two hours; one of fifteen pounds, two hours and a half. The greatest care must be taken that it only just simmers the whole of the time.

Take it out of the cloth, remove the bacon, and pull out the skewers. Place the turkey on a hot dish. – NOTE – Reserve the liquor in an earthen uncovered pot for soup.

Don't forget about first soaking the tongue. In my experience a straightforward brined or pickled tongue will need a minimum of 12–18 hours soaking in a large bowl of cold water, changed at least once; a smoked tongue, which is drier, harder and more shrunken, needs up to 48 hours steeping, the water changed twice. To boil an average-size pickled or smoked tongue takes 3½–5 hours of gentle simmering. If possible, skin and trim while still warm.

⭢ ESCALOPES OF TURKEY WITH MUSHROOMS ⭠
As an alternative to facing the cold remains of a roast turkey for days on end, a household of two or three can enjoy it first in this very delicate dish, and a day or two later in a cassoulet.

For the escalopes, carve the breast (uncooked) into fillets, and flatten them a little as for an escalope of veal. Season with salt and pepper, dip them in beaten egg, then in fine fresh white bread crumbs, doing the operation twice so that they have a double coating.

In a heavy sauté pan melt about 3oz of butter and cook the escalopes in it gently, turning them over two or three times and keeping the pan covered in the intervals; they will take 20–30 minutes to cook, according to the quality of the turkey.

Ten minutes before they are ready, sauté ½lb of small mushrooms in butter in another pan. Arrange the turkey and the mushrooms in the serving dish and keep them hot.

To the butter in the first pan add a small glass of brandy and set a light to it. Cook for another 30 seconds after the flames have died down, and serve the sauce separately.

→ TURKEY BREASTS FRIED WITH HAM AND CHEESE ←

Cut the breast of not-too-large a turkey into fillets. An 8lb turkey should give 8–10 good-sized fillets. Flatten them out a little on a wooden board, season them with salt and pepper and dust them very lightly with flour.

Melt a generous amount of butter in a frying-pan (if they are all to be done at once you will probably need to keep two pans going at the same time). Cook the fillets on both sides, gently, for the butter must not blacken or burn. When they have cooked 10 minutes place a slice of ham on each fillet, and then a layer of grated Parmesan cheese of the best quality obtainable. Over each fillet pour a tablespoon of chicken or turkey broth. Cover the pan. Proceed to cook very gently for another 7–10 minutes. Some of the cheese will spread and amalgamate with the butter and the stock in the pan to form a sauce. Serve quickly, for if the dish is kept waiting the sauce will dry up and the cheese will become hard.

✄ VARIATION: TURKEY BREASTS WITH MARSALA ✄

Another way of serving the turkey breasts is to start them off in butter, in the same way, and then add a small glass of Marsala; after this has bubbled and amalgamated with the butter, add the same quantity of broth. Cook in the open pan another 2 or 3 minutes.

→ TURKEY STEWED IN WHITE WINE ←
A dish to make with the rest of the turkey when the breast has been cooked as above.

The other ingredients are 1 onion, butter, salt and pepper, flour, 2 carrots, a small turnip, garlic, a small slice of ham or bacon, herbs, half a lemon, ½ pint of white wine, 1½ pints of turkey or chicken stock, half a teacup of fresh bread crumbs, ½ lb of fresh mushrooms or 1 oz of dried ones.

Cut the turkey into joints. Fry the chopped onion in butter in a commodious pan. Salt and pepper the pieces of turkey and flour them lightly. Brown them in the butter with the onion. Put in the chopped carrots, turnip and garlic, diced ham or bacon, herbs, and the half lemon. Pour over the white wine and let it cook, not too fast, for 10 minutes, stirring from time to time. Add the stock. Cover the pan and cook for about 1½ hours – longer if the turkey is a large one.

Strain off all the liquid and keep the pieces of turkey hot in the oven. Put the liquid and the vegetables, bacon and lemon through a sieve. To this purée add the bread crumbs and the mushrooms (if dried ones are used they should be previously soaked for 10 minutes in warm water). Cook the sauce for 10 minutes, stirring it so as to amalgamate the bread crumbs, which serve to thicken the sauce. Pour it back over the turkey and let it all get thoroughly well heated before serving.

Plain boiled rice goes well with this dish.

✣ CASSOULET OF TURKEY ✣

The day before you are going to make the cassoulet, put 1lb (for three or four people) of dried haricot beans to soak in water. Prepare also about 4 pints of stock from the carcass and giblets of the turkey, with carrots, onions, herbs and celery.

The next day put the turkey, cut into joints, into the bottom of a deep earthenware pot; add up to 1lb of bacon (or a ham bone, bacon bones, or a piece of uncooked salami sausage). Put the strained beans on top, with a chopped onion, 2 or 3 chopped fresh tomatoes, 2 chopped cloves of garlic, a little salt, ground black pepper, a bay leaf and some thyme or marjoram. Cover, a good inch above the top of the beans, with the strained turkey stock, put the lid on the casserole and cook in a slow oven, 325°F, for 3–4 hours, until the beans are tender and the stock nearly all absorbed.

Sausages can be added to the dish half an hour before serving. If the cassoulet is to be made with the legs and wings of previously cooked turkey, add them to the beans only half an hour before serving.

✣ GRATIN OF TURKEY IN CREAM SAUCE ✣
This is a really worthwhile dish to make with some of the turkey meat; it's a dish I often make from a chicken cooked especially for the purpose, because the creamy, cheese-flavored sauce with the chicken makes such a soothing, gentle combination of flavors

and textures. That is to say, it does if the sauce really is
creamy and if there is rather a lot of it in proportion to
the chicken or turkey meat.

Ingredients for a dish for three or four people are about ¾ lb
of cooked turkey or chicken weighed when it has been taken
from the bone and, for the sauce, 1½ oz of butter, 2 tablespoons of flour, ½ pint of milk, 4 tablespoons each of stock
from the bird and cream or, if there is no stock, 8 tablespoons
of cream. Seasonings include nutmeg as well as salt and
freshly milled pepper and 3 tablespoons of grated Parmesan
or Gruyère, plus a little extra, with bread crumbs, for the
final cooking of the dish.

Melt the butter in a thick saucepan, put in the flour, stir it
round, off the fire, until it forms a smooth paste; add a little
of the warmed milk. Return to the fire and stir while you add
the rest of the milk. When the sauce is smooth and thick add
the stock, cream and seasonings; there should be a good measure of pepper and nutmeg but only a very little salt until after
the cheese has been added. It may then be necessary to add
more. At this stage put the saucepan into another large one
containing water and let it cook in this bain-marie, stirring
frequently, for a good 20 minutes. Now add the cheese and
stir again until it has amalgamated with the sauce. Remove
all skin and sinew from the turkey or chicken, cut it into thin
strips, as much of a size as possible.

Cover the bottom of a shallow gratin dish with a thin layer
of the sauce. Put in the turkey or chicken in one layer. Cover
it completely with the rest of the sauce. Sprinkle with bread
crumbs and grated cheese and cook for about 15 minutes in
a moderate oven, 350°F, and then transfer it to the grill for a
minute or two and serve it when the top is just beginning to

blister into golden bubbles. If you do this gratin in larger quantities, use a dish in proportion. It will not be good if it is squashed into too small a space.

✣ Salmis de Dinde à la Berrichonne ✣
This is a good way of dealing with a turkey neither young nor tender.

First of all prepare a stock with the giblets, neck and feet of the turkey, browned in butter with an onion, a carrot, a clove of garlic, thyme, bay leaf and parsley. Sprinkle with a tablespoon of flour and let it turn golden, then add a glass of red wine and two of water and leave to simmer for an hour.

In the meantime cut up the turkey, dividing the legs and wings into 2 pieces each and the breast into 4 pieces. Season them with salt and pepper. Put 3oz of butter into a casserole or braising pan and when it is melted put in the pieces of turkey; let them turn golden on each side; take them out and keep them aside.

Into the same butter put ¼lb of bacon cut into small squares and 1lb of small mushrooms. When these in their turn have browned, take them out, and to the butter and juices in the pan add a glass of red wine and let it simmer 2 or 3 minutes, then add the prepared stock, through a strainer.

Put back the pieces of turkey, covered with the bacon and the mushrooms, and add 2 tablespoons of brandy. Cover the pan and cook very slowly for 1½–2 hours. Serve garnished with triangles of fried bread.

→ SALTED GOOSE ←

Robert May, a professional cook and son of a professional cook, published what became one of the most famous of all English cookery books, *The Accomplisht Cook*. He was born in 1588, and from his father, then as apprentice to Arthur Hollingsworth, cook to the Grocers' Hall and the Star Chamber, learned the dishes that were already traditional in the mid-sixteenth century. It is this point that makes his recipes of exceptional historical interest. Having worked in a number of grand and noble households, he was accustomed to lavish entertainments and the preparation of banquets and feasts, so we can take it that his list of forty Christmas dishes, and the manner of their service in two courses, each one in itself a banquet, is representative of the kind of festive food served during late Tudor times and the first, pre-Cromwell, Stuart era.

A particularly interesting item in May's Christmas fare is his powdered goose, powdered meaning salted or pickled. Salting of geese was evidently taken for granted, for May gives no specific instructions for the brine or pickle, but "being powdered" the goose was stuffed with a mixture of oatmeal steeped in warm milk, then mixed with beef suet, onions and apples, the whole seasoned with cloves and mace, sweet herbs and pepper. The goose was then boiled and served with a "brewes" (broth) and "colliflowers, cabbidge, turnips and barberries" and "beaten butter."

In a little booklet entitled *Dorset Dishes of the Eighteenth Century*, edited by J. Stevens Cox, and published by the Dorset National History and Archaeological Society in 1961, appears a more specific recipe for a salted and smoked goose. It comes, the editor tells us, from the Recipe Book of Judith Frampton of Morton House, near Dorchester, dated 1708.

> Take the fairest and fattest goose you can get and dry him well within, take out the soul [that is, the black spongy part adhering to the back of the goose] then take some bay salt and beat it well and salt him well and let him lye a fortnight in salt, then tye him up in paper and hang him up in Chimney where they burn woode or coale, let him hang a fortnight or three weekes in that time he will be readye to boyle you may keep him for longer if you please before you boyle him.

From Sir Harry Luke author of the *Tenth Muse*, an entrancing book of recipes and kitchen wisdom first published in 1954, come more practical instructions as to the pickling and cooking of a goose. This, definitely, is one to be tried.

> A goose, seven ounces sugar, two ounces saltpeter, three pounds salt.
>
> Boil up five quarts water with the saltpeter, sugar and salt, and pour hot over the goose, which has been cleaned and trussed; leave the goose lying in this decoction for three days, then boil slowly until tender.
>
> The goose should be served cold with a sauce made of lightly whipped cream in which are mixed white vinegar, grated horse-

radish and a pinch of sugar. The sauce should be frozen in the refrigerator before serving. (A specialty from the Southern Swedish province of Scania.)

→ GOOSE WITH CHESTNUTS AND APPLES ←

The chestnuts and apples are prepared like a stuffing, but they don't go into the goose, they are cooked separately. This is because if you are going to have your goose cold, a stuffing is too fat-soaked from the bird to be attractive, whereas if it is baked separately in a terrine or a pie dish it comes out almost like a pâté and can be cut into nice even slices as an accompaniment, and all you will probably need besides is a big bowl of salad (endive, celery, and beetroot is a good one) and baked potatoes for those who have given up caring about their weight.

To start on the chestnuts – about 1½lb. Score them right across on the rounded side, preferably with a broken-off, but still sharp knife which isn't going to be ruined in the process. Put them in a baking tin, half at a time, and cook them in a moderate oven for 10–15 minutes. Take out a few and, to shell and skin them, squeeze each nut in your hand so that the shell bursts. Then it comes off quite easily with the aid of a sharp knife, sometimes bringing the inner skin with it, sometimes not. And if this inner skin will not come away easily, leave it, do not hack at it. When all except these resistant ones are done, put them in a basin and pour boiling water over them. This should succeed in loosening the skins. Put the chestnuts in a saucepan with ½ pint of milk and 4 table-spoons of water and simmer them for about half an hour, until they are quite soft.

Meanwhile peel, slice and core 4 sweet apples, and stew them in a little water until they are almost in a purée. Drain the liquid from the chestnuts, break them up roughly but do not mash them. Mix them with the apples, add ¼lb of minced lean veal, 2 finely chopped shallots, 2 tablespoons of parsley, a very little salt, freshly milled pepper, and a well-beaten egg. Turn into a buttered pie dish or terrine, which you put, covered with a buttered paper, into the oven at the same time as the goose, and take out after about 1½ hours.

If you have bought your goose a day or two before you intend to cook it, it will benefit from being well rubbed with coarse salt night and morning, left in a cool larder, and the salt carefully wiped off before cooking. But if the weather is muggy this procedure is not advisable. Most Christmas birds have been killed a good deal in advance and once out of the poulterers' cold rooms are best cooked as soon as possible, unless your refrigerator is large enough to hold them.

Put the goose on a rack in the largest baking tin which will get into the oven. Cover it with an oiled paper or foil, and bake it 2½–3 hours for a goose weighing about 8lb at 325°F. During the final half hour turn the heat very low and remove the paper so that the skin turns golden.

The fat from the bird should be separated from the juices and poured off into a bowl, for it is very valuable for frying; the juices can be mixed with wine-flavored stock from the giblets to make a sauce for the goose.

→ ROAST GOOSE WITH POTATOES ←
To roast a goose successfully a capacious, deep roasting tin is necessary to catch the large amount of fat which flows from the bird during cooking.

As there are plenty of potatoes to go with it, the goose need not be stuffed. It is covered with buttered paper or foil and is cooked standing on a grid placed in the baking tin. This is important. If the goose is put straight into the tin it will stew in its fat and be greasy. After the first hour, take it from the oven and pour off most of the fat in the tin. Put in 2–3lb of partly cooked potatoes cut into quarters, all the same size. By the time the goose is cooked the potatoes should be tender and deliciously flavored with the fat from the bird. Ten minutes before serving add to the potatoes 4 or 5 hard-boiled eggs cut in quarters, which will also become golden and slightly crackling from the goose fat. Arrange the potatoes and eggs, drained of excess fat, all round the goose on the serving dish, and put a bunch of watercress at each end.

Cooking time is 2½–3 hours in a rather low oven, 325°F, turned down to very low for the last hour, with the paper removed so that the skin becomes crisp and golden.

Good though the above method is, I cannot help agreeing with the author of one of my favorite French cookery books, *Clarisse, ou la Vieille Cuisinière*, that the goose, being to other poultry what pork is to butcher's meat, is at its best served cold, like all very fat meats. And nowadays many people have sensibly come round to the idea of cooking their Christmas bird the day before and thereby avoiding some at least of the last-minute confusion and anxiety. By the time a large bird is carved and served it is usually tepid anyway, and a properly cooled bird is altogether more desirable.

Be sure to save the fat from the goose. It is valuable for many dishes. As for the liver, there is little use in English cooks indulging in fantasies about *pâté de foie gras* or similar delicacies, for the liver of an English goose will weigh at the most about 4oz, whereas those of the specially fattened geese of

Alsace and the Périgord often weigh as much as 2lb or more. The dish of chicken livers with rice described below provides a good way of using up both goose and turkey livers.

✣ Goose Giblet Stew ✣

A rich and savory stew can be made from the goose giblets. This recipe is from southwestern France.

Slice 2 or 3 large onions. Fry them very gently in a little goose fat. When they are pale golden, put in all the giblets except the liver, and a 6oz slice of salt pork or gammon. Let them take color, add 3 or 4 sliced carrots, 3 large tomatoes, plenty of garlic, salt, pepper and a big bouquet of herbs.

Pour over ½ pint of heated stock. Bring to simmering point; cover the pot; cook in a very low oven, 275°F, for 2½–3 hours. Serve with boiled white haricot beans, augmented if you like with a well-spiced, coarsely cut sausage.

✣ Roast Capon, and Tomatoes with Rice ✣
and Walnut Stuffing

Put a lump of butter worked with tarragon or parsley inside a 3½lb capon, rub the bird generously with butter, stand it on a grid in a baking tin and roast it slowly on its side in the center of a very moderate oven, 325°F, for 1½ hours altogether, turning it over at half-time, then breast upward for the final 10 minutes, and basting from time to time with melted butter (about 2oz) warmed in a little pan on top of the stove. Add a couple of tablespoons of white wine to the buttery juices in the pan, let them bubble a minute or two over a fast flame and serve in a sauceboat. A plain giblet gravy as an alternative to the rich buttery one can be prepared the day before by cooking the giblets with an unpeeled onion, a sliced tomato, a small piece of celery, 2 or 3 sprigs of parsley, and water just to cover. This needs about 3 hours' extremely slow cooking, and is best done in the oven. Then all you have to do is to strain the gravy, season it, and heat it up and reduce it a little when the capon is ready.

For 8–10 large tomatoes, the ingredients for the stuffing are 3oz of rice, a chopped shallot, 2oz of shelled and chopped walnuts, a dessertspoon of currants, the grated peel of half a lemon, 1oz of butter, pepper, salt, nutmeg and 1 egg, a little olive oil or extra melted butter. Boil the rice, keeping it slightly underdone. Drain and while still warm mix it with all the other ingredients. Slice off the tops of the tomatoes, scoop out the pulp, add it to the rice mixture, fill the tomatoes, piling the stuffing up into a mound, replace the tops, put them in an oiled baking tin or dish, pour a few drops of oil or melted butter over each and bake in the oven while the capon is cooking: about half an hour should be sufficient.

❖ Roast Pheasant with Chestnut Sauce ❖

A young but fully grown pheasant will weigh about 1½lb and takes approximately 45 minutes to roast. Put a lump of butter inside the bird, wrap it in well-buttered paper, place it on its side on a grid standing in a baking tin and cook in the center of a preheated fairly hot oven, 375°F.

Turn it over after the first 20 minutes, after another 15 minutes remove the paper and turn the bird breast upward for the last 10 minutes.

For the chestnut sauce, which can be made a day or two in advance and slowly reheated, the ingredients are ½lb of chestnuts, 1½oz of butter, 2 sticks of celery, 1 rasher of bacon, about 6 tablespoons of port, salt, a little cream or stock.

Score the chestnuts on one side, bake them in a moderate oven, 350°F, for 15 minutes, shell and skin them. Chop them roughly. Heat the butter, put in the chopped celery and bacon, add the chestnuts, the port, an equal quantity of water, and a very little salt. Cover the saucepan and cook very gently for about 30 minutes until the chestnuts are quite tender. When reheating, enrich the mixture with a couple of tablespoons of rich meat or game stock or double cream.

This mixture is fairly solid, really more like a vegetable dish than a sauce proper, but whatever you like to call it, it goes to perfection with pheasant. A good creamy bread sauce or simply crisp bread crumbs put in a baking tin with a little butter and left in the oven for about 15–20 minutes could provide an alternative, and personally I always like a few fried or baked chipolata sausages with a pheasant. If you prefer to have your pheasant cold, a bowl of those beautiful Italian fruits in mustard syrup would be better than the chestnut sauce. And have a hot first course, an egg dish perhaps (a spoonful of the tomato fondue described in the recipe for Baked Fillet of Beef, with a little cream, added to baked eggs is a good one); or some scallops, or a creamy vegetable soup.

⇥ OVEN-POACHED CHICKEN ⇤

A wonderfully easy way of cooking a roasting chicken to be eaten cold during the days before Christmas, the carcass

coming in useful to make a stock that could be the basis of
the simple "Tomato Consommé."

Ingredients are 1 roasting chicken, approximately 3½lb, 2
carrots, 1 small turnip, a couple of celery stalks, 6 coriander
seeds, 6 little slices of fresh ginger, salt, and water for poach-
ing the chicken. Optionally, a tablespoon of sherry. Mind: no
onion or garlic.

Put the prepared chicken in a cocotte or casserole in which
it will just fit. Surround it with the vegetables and aromatics.
Add a scant tablespoon of the sherry if you are using it, salt,
and water just to cover.

Cover the chicken with foil and the lid of the casserole and
cook it low down in the oven at 300°F, for just one hour.

Take out the chicken and leave it to cool, covered with a
cloth. Filter the broth through muslin and refrigerate it. Have
the cold chicken with Lemon and Celery Sauce, or use the
breast and wings to make A White Chicken Cream (see "First
Courses.")

→ COLD POACHED CHICKEN WITH CREAM SAUCE ←
For a buffet lunch or supper this makes a mild, soothing dish;
it takes time to prepare but the result is rewarding.

Ingredients are a large boiling chicken weighing about 5lb, 2
carrots, an onion, a piece of celery, a bunch of parsley, salt,
6oz of Patna or Italian rice, freshly ground pepper, nutmeg
and lemon juice; and for the sauce 2oz of butter, 2 full tablespoons of flour, ¼ pint each of milk and single cream, 1–1½
pints of the liquid in which the chicken was cooked, a little
fresh tarragon.

Put the chicken, with the giblets, in a big pan (one which

will go in the oven) with the sliced carrots and onion, the celery and parsley tied together, a tablespoon of salt, and water just to cover (if you have some to spare, it is an improvement to add a glass of white wine or cider). Bring gently to simmering point on top of the stove, skim, cover the pot closely and transfer it to a moderate oven, 325°F, and cook for just about 3 hours. Remove the chicken to a dish and let it cool. Discard the vegetables. Strain the stock into a bowl.

To make the sauce, melt the butter in a heavy saucepan; off the fire stir in the flour and when it is smooth add first the heated milk, then gradually 1 pint of the chicken stock. Stir until smooth, simmer very gently, with a mat under the saucepan, for about 30 minutes, stirring frequently. Add the cream. Continue simmering and stirring another 5 minutes or so. If the sauce is too thick add a little more stock, and if it is still too runny let it cook and reduce a little longer. Strain the sauce through a fine sieve into a jug, taste for seasoning, stir in about a teaspoon of chopped tarragon, cover the sauce with a piece of buttered paper and leave until the next day.

Boil the rice, drain it, and while it is still warm season it with salt, pepper, nutmeg, lemon juice. Spread it out on a long dish.

Remove the skin from the chicken, take all the meat from the bones, cut it into rather small longish pieces. Mix the chicken with the sauce, but keep aside one cupful of the latter. Arrange the chicken and sauce mixture on top of the rice. Some of the sauce will seep through into the rice and make it just sufficiently moist. Just before serving cover the chicken with the reserved sauce and sprinkle with a little chopped parsley or tarragon.

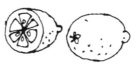

→ La Poule au Riz à la Crème ←

*Coming as a first course in a farmhouse supper (see "Christmas
in France") a poule au riz would most likely consist of the broth
from the bird thickened with rice, with the chicken cut up and
served separately; but there are many other ways of preparing
this mild and soothing dish which, well-known though it is,
requires rather careful preparation and a well-made creamy
sauce if it is to be presented at its best.*

Supposing it is to be made with a boiling chicken weighing
4–5lb, the other ingredients are ¼lb of fat unsmoked bacon
or salt breast of pork, 2 onions, 3 or 4 carrots, bouquet of herbs,
and garlic; if possible approximately 4 pints of stock made
from the giblets plus a piece of knuckle of veal; and very good
quality rice. And for the sauce, butter, flour, stock from the
chicken, 8oz of cream, 2 egg yolks, lemon, with finely chopped
parsley and tarragon to finish.

Line the bottom of a heavy oval pan with the bacon or salt
pork cut in very thin slices. On top put the chicken, with its
own fat or a piece of butter rolled in salt and pepper inside,
rubbed with lemon on the outside. Surround it with the sliced
onions and carrots. Start it on a moderate fire and let it cook
gently about 10–15 minutes until the fat is running and a
faint smell of frying comes from the pan; pour in the heated
stock, of which there should be enough completely to cover
the legs of the bird but not the breast; if there is not sufficient, make it up with water. (If you already have stock from
a previously cooked chicken instead of having to make it specially, so much the better.)

Put in a big bouquet of fresh parsley, bay leaves, a crushed
clove of garlic and some sprigs of thyme or marjoram. Let
the stock come to simmering point, add just a little salt. Cover

the pot with buttered paper and a close-fitting lid. Transfer to a moderate oven, 350°F, and allow half an hour to 1lb.

About 45 minutes before serving time start off the rice, which is to be what the French call *riz au gras*, moist rather than fluffy, but still with all the grains separate. For 4 people allow about ¾lb; having weighed it, measure it in a cup or glass, and then calculate twice its volume in stock, which is to be taken from the pot in which the chicken is cooking. Put your rice into a big pan of boiling salted water and cook it about 7 minutes, boiling fairly fast. Drain it, hold the colander under the cold tap until the water that runs out is quite clear. Put the rice in a pot or pan which will go into the oven. Extract the required amount of stock from the chicken (at this moment turn the bird over in its liquid) and pour it over the rice. Bring to simmering point on top of the stove. Put a folded cloth on top, cover with the lid and put in the oven to finish cooking. It will be perfectly cooked, all the liquid absorbed, in about 25 minutes, but a little longer will do no harm.

For the sauce: melt 1oz of butter in a saucepan, stir in 2 tablespoons of flour and about ½ pint of hot stock, which can have been taken from the chicken at the same time as that for the rice. Stir until you have a smooth, thickish sauce. Add your cream (single cream will be all right) and leave it to cook very gently, stirring from time to time to prevent a skin forming. Season if necessary with salt; beat the egg yolks with a little lemon juice and stir them into the sauce. Keep another minute or two over the fire, add the chopped parsley and tarragon (dried when no fresh is available), and then put the saucepan into another one containing hot water, so that it does not boil again.

To serve: carve the bird, pour the sauce over the pieces, and serve the rice either separately in a large warmed dish, or arranged all round the chicken. A young roasting chicken can be prepared in exactly the same way, except that it will need a good deal less cooking – not more than 15 minutes to 1lb. The dish then becomes a *poularde*, instead of a *poule au riz*.

✣ Chicken Livers with Rice ✦

Prepare a dish of *riz au gras* in the way described above, using about ½lb of rice.

Slice ½lb of very carefully cleaned chicken livers into 2 or 3 pieces each. Season them and dust them with flour. Cook them gently a minute or two in foaming butter with 1–2oz of chopped cooked ham. Pour in 2 or 3 tablespoons of white wine or Madeira or white vermouth. Let it bubble and reduce. Add 3 tablespoons of the same stock which has been used for the rice. Cook another couple of minutes.

Turn out the rice on to a heated serving dish, and put the chicken livers in a mound on the top. Sprinkle with a little parsley. Enough for four as a first course.

✣ Swedish Salt Duck ✦
This is a great and simple delicacy, very similar to our own Welsh salt duck and perhaps even better, owing to the method of salting and to the inclusion of a very small proportion of saltpeter with the salt. This subtly alters the flavor and gives the flesh of the cooked duck an appetizing pink tinge.

For one large duck weighing approximately 4½lb, the only other ingredients needed are 6oz of rock salt, a scant teaspoon of saltpeter, and water.

Amalgamate the salt and saltpeter very thoroughly. Fill a large shallow baking tin or earthenware oven dish with cold water. Place a roasting rack, cake-cooling tray, or simply three strips of wood across the water-filled dish.

Rub a one-third portion of the salt mixture into the duck and put some also into the cavity, and place the duck, breast upward, on the rack, so that it is as close to the water as possible without touching it. Cover the duck with a light cloth and leave it in a cool place.

Every 12 hours or so for 36–48 hours, repeat the rubbing-in process with the salt mixture, each time renewing the water underneath. The idea – and it works – is that the water attracts the salt and melts it, accelerating the penetration of the salt into the duck flesh.

When the salt mixture is used up, and the duck has been salted for 2½ or 3 days, simply place the duck, breast upward and uncovered, in the baking dish, fill this with fresh cold water, and put it on the center shelf of a very low oven, 300°F. In exactly 2 hours the duck will be cooked. Take it from the water, leave it to cool on a rack placed over a dish, and serve it cold and carved into fine slices. Cooked in this way, salt duck is so delicate that although in Sweden there would be a horseradish and cream sauce, or a sweet mustard sauce to go with it, I find it best with an extremely simple salad made from cubes of honeydew melon with a very little lemon juice.

⇨ Duck Baked in Cider ⇦

Rub a 6lb duck thoroughly with about ¼lb of coarse salt; leave it with its salt in a deep dish for 24 hours, turning it once or twice and rubbing the salt well in. To cook it, wash off the salt with cold water. In a deep baking dish or enameled tin with a cover (such as a self-basting roasting pan) put a couple of carrots, an unpeeled onion, a clove of garlic, a bouquet of herbs, and the giblets but not the liver of the duck. Place the duck on top of the vegetables, pour over about I pint of dry vintage cider, and then fill up with water barely to cover the duck. Put the lid on the pan, stand this pan in a tin of water, cook in a very slow oven, 300°F, for just about 2 hours.

If to be served hot, take the cover off the pan during the final 15 minutes' cooking, so that the skin of the duck is baked a beautiful pale golden brown. If to be served cold, which is perhaps even better, leave it to cool for half an hour or so in its cooking liquid before taking it out. The flavor of this duck is so good that only the simplest of salads is required to go with it, or perhaps the Sweet-Sour Cherry Sauce from the "Sauces, Pickles and Chutney" chapter. The stock, strained, with fat removed, makes a splendid basis for mushroom or lentil soup.

❊ Traditional Christmas Dishes ❊

How the food of a past age tasted seems to us almost impossible to imagine. We know roughly what our ancestors' kitchens were like, what sort of pots they cooked in and what fuel they used. We have their cookery books and recipes and ample evidence of how their meals were composed. All this still doesn't convey to us what the food tasted like to them.

The reproduction of dishes cooked precisely according to the recipes of 100 or 200 years ago is a fairly pointless undertaking, not only because our tastes, our methods of cookery and our equipment have so totally changed but because even the identical ingredients would no longer taste the same. Period clothes for the stage inevitably bear the stamp of contemporary fashion, however much trouble the designers and the cutters have taken over the authentic detail. So it is with food. And I always feel a bit dubious when I read about traditional English puddings and pies, cakes and creams, pickles, hams, cheeses and preserves being made "precisely according to a 300-year-old recipe." Even were this really so, I can't help thinking our ancestors would have considerable difficulty in recognizing them. *Chemical feeding stuffs and new systems of breeding and fattening animals for market, vegetables and fruit grown in artificially fertilized soil, the pasteurizing of milk and cream, the production of eggs from battery hens, the refining of salt and flour, the substitution of beet sugar for cane, the preservation of fish by modern methods, and even the chlorination of water – in what way these developments have caused our food to deteriorate or to improve is not under discussion here, but certainly they have changed the nature of almost every single ingredient that comes into our kitchens.*

In La Cuisine de Tous les Mois, *a cookery book published in the 1890s by Philéas Gilbert, a great teaching chef and one of Escoffier's collaborators, is to be found the following very relevant observation.* "Cookery," says Gilbert, "is as old as the world, but it must also remain, always, as modern as fashion." *And as Christmas is the season when rather more improbable talk than usual goes on about what is called "traditional English fare," I have tried to take Philéas Gilbert's hint and to produce recipes which, while based on the old ones, are modern in treatment. It is a system which works so long as the spirit of the recipes is preserved, for then we do get some sense of a continuing tradition into our cookery, avoiding the farcical effect produced by "traditional" recipes made up almost entirely of synthetic or substitute ingredients. I have not forgotten that recipe sent out a few years ago by a publicity firm and said by them to have been dropped by Richard the Third's cook on the field of Bosworth. (A careless crowd, Richard and his followers.) By a fascinating coincidence this recipe called for the use of a highly advertised brand of modern vegetable cooking lard.*

On the other hand, methods, quantities, and, especially, seasonings, have to be modernized, or all we get is a sort of folk-weave cooking perilously close to that hilarious land of which Miss Joyce Grenfell is queen, with the American advertisements of the British Travel Association for hand-maidens.

Meat

────────── ⊰ · VI · ⊱ ──────────

✣ Spiced Beef for Christmas ✣

Dry-pickled or spiced beef is very different in flavor from the brine-pickled or salt beef sold by the butchers. It used to be a regular Christmas dish in a great many English country houses and farms. "This is more a Christmas dish than any other time of the year," says John Simpson, cook to the Marquis of Buckingham, in his Complete System of Cookery *(1806), "not but it may be done any time, and is equally good." He calls it rather grandly* Bœuf de Chasse, *but under the names of Hunting Beef, or* Beef à l'Écarlate, *or simply Spiced Beef, various forms of the recipe have certainly been known for at least three hundred years.*

In former times huge rounds of beef weighing upwards of 20lb were required to lie in pickle for 3–4 weeks. A 5–12lb piece will, however, be ready for cooking after 10–14 days.

HERE ARE TWO prescriptions for the spices worked out for varying quantities of meat. The presence of juniper berries among the pickling spices makes the recipe somewhat unusual. They appear in old recipes from Yorkshire, Cumberland, Wales, Sussex – those areas, in fact, where the juniper shrub grows wild on the hills. The dried berries can be bought from grocers who specialize in spices, and from any of the small kitchen shops which now sell herbs and spices.

TABLE

For a 10–12lb joint		For a 5–6lb joint
5–6oz	light brown Barbados or other brown cane sugar	3oz
1oz	saltpeter	½oz
6oz	sea or rock salt	4oz
2oz	black peppercorns	1oz
1oz	allspice berries (also known as pimento and Jamaica pepper; to be bought from the same shops as the juniper berries)	½oz
2oz	juniper berries	1oz

Ask the butcher for the best-quality round or silverside beef and explain to him what it is for. He will probably be incredulous but will know how to cut and skewer it.

First rub the beef all over with the brown sugar and leave it for 2 days in a glazed stoneware crock or bowl. Crush all the spices, with the salt and saltpeter, in a mortar. They should be well broken up but need not be reduced to a powder. With this mixture you rub the beef thoroughly each day for 9–14 days according to the size. Gradually, with the salt and sugar, the beef produces a certain amount of its own liquid, and it smells most appetizing. But keep it covered, and in a cool airy place, not in a stuffy kitchen.

When the time comes to cook the beef, take it from the

crock, rinse off any of the spices which are adhering to it, but without sousing the meat in cold water.

Put it in a big deep cast-iron pot, preferably oval, in which it fits with very little space to spare. Pour in about ½ pint of water. In the old days the meat would now have been covered with shredded suet to keep in the moisture, then with a thick crust made from flour and lard, but the suet and the sealing crust can both be dispensed with, two or three layers of grease-proof paper or foil being used instead, to make sure there is no evaporation of juices. Put the lid on the pot. Bake in a very low oven, 275°F, for 5 hours for the smaller joint, 7½ hours for the larger. Take it from the oven carefully, for there will be a certain amount of liquid round the beef. Leave it to cool for 2–3 hours. But before the fat sets, pour off all the liquid and remove the beef to a board. Wrap it in foil or greaseproof paper and put another board or a plate on top, and a 2–4lb weight. Leave it until next day.

The beef will carve thinly and evenly, and has a rich, mellow, spicy flavor which does seem to convey to us some sort of idea of the food eaten by our forebears. Once cooked the beef will keep fresh for several days, in an ordinary larder provided it is kept wrapped in clean greaseproof paper frequently renewed. It can also be stored in a refrigerator so long as it is taken out and kept at room temperature for a couple of hours or so before it is to be eaten.

→ BAKED FILLET OF BEEF WITH TOMATO FONDUE ←
Fillet is not a cut I often buy; it is expensive and always has to be ordered in advance because there is such a big demand for it and only a small piece in each animal, and then one gets so sick and tired of the fillet steaks, which are often the only safe thing to order in restaurants. But Christmas weekend, when so many families are

buying poultry, hams, gammons, spiced beef and legs of pork instead
of the usual weekend joint, is a good moment to try for a really
fine piece of fillet. It is so easy to cook and carve, and provides
such an excellent contrast to cloying Christmas food.

Suppose you have a fillet weighing about 2½lb, which should provide two meals for four people, all you have to do is to brush the joint with olive oil or melted beef dripping, stand it on a grid in a baking tin, put it in the center of a preheated moderately hot oven, 375°F. There you leave it, without basting or turning it over or paying the slightest attention to it for 45 minutes to an hour, according to whether you want it very underdone or only moderately so. You put it on a long hot serving dish (let it stand a few minutes before carving) with watercress at each end, and, separately, serve the following tomato fondue, which can be made in advance if it's more convenient and then gently heated up.

In a small saucepan heat 1½oz of butter. In this melt 2 finely sliced shallots or 1 very small onion; add 4 large skinned and chopped tomatoes, a seasoning of very little salt, nutmeg and dried basil. Cook gently for a quarter of an hour. Add 1 tablespoon of brandy or Armagnac and simmer slowly another 10 minutes. Finally, add a tablespoon of Madeira, a little chopped parsley, a small lump of butter and the small quantity of juices which have come from the meat; the fondue is ready.

But if you feel like an extravagance buy a small tin or jar of black truffles, add the juice from the tin at the same time as the brandy, then the sliced truffles. Serve in a little sauce tureen. And as an alternative choice for a guest with traditional tastes, have either some horseradish sauce as well, or plenty of parsley butter, and potatoes, either plain boiled – or, easier still because they won't get overcooked while you aren't

looking – boil the potatoes in advance, keeping them somewhat underdone, cut them in quarters and bake them with
butter or beef dripping in a shallow dish in the oven while the
beef is cooking.

Either with or after the beef, a very simple salad of Belgian
endives sliced into ½ inch chunks, with an ordinary dressing
of olive oil and wine vinegar or lemon juice to which a pinch
of sugar as well as salt and pepper is added, will be very welcome. Then cheese, perhaps a beautiful piece of Lancashire
instead of the conventional Stilton, and fruit.

✣ ESTOUFFAT DE BŒUF ALBIGEOIS ✣

This sumptuously flavored old-fashioned daube *of southwestern
France was the kind of dish that could be left cooking all night
long in a sealed pot in the dying embers of the farmhouse hearth, or
in earlier days in the gradually cooling brick oven after the bread
had been baked. I don't suppose you'd find it very often these days,
but that's no reason for not cooking it here. The lengthy cooking
produces a beautifully tender piece of meat and a rich but rather fat
sauce – to counteract this, serve it with plain boiled potatoes or rice.
It is also delicious cold. Made during the week before or the
week after Christmas, it is a splendid dish to serve cold
on Christmas or New Year's Eve.*

To make it you need a fine large piece of topside or top rump
of beef. It isn't really worth making it with less than 4–5lb.
Other ingredients are 4 or 5 tablespoons of olive oil, 4 or 5
carrots, 2 large cloves of garlic, an onion or two if you like
(I don't, and find the ultimate flavor far finer without it), about
1lb of streaky salt pork or fresh pork belly if you have no salt
pork, or unsmoked bacon but not smoked bacon, 2 pig's trotters, split by the butcher, a big bunch of aromatic herbs – dried

wild thyme, bay leaves, a strip of orange peel – at least ½ a bottle of red wine, a large glass (about 4fl oz) of brandy or Armagnac, salt and pepper. For cooking the *estouffat* you need a large earthenware or cast-iron pot with a well-fitting lid.

Have your beef rolled and tied in a good shape. Rub a little salt all over it. Warm the olive oil in the casserole, put in the meat, let it brown gently. Add the scrubbed but unpeeled carrots, the crushed garlic cloves, the sliced onions if you are using them, the salt pork cut into small pieces, the split trotters, the bunch of herbs. If you are using an earthenware pot heat the red wine before pouring it in (cold liquid poured into a hot dryish pot will crack it). Let it bubble a minute or two, then add the brandy. Don't flame it. The *estouffat* is going to cook for so long that there is no need for preliminary evaporation of alcohol. Add salt and pepper.

Cover the pot. Transfer it to a very low oven, 300°F. Leave it for at least 5 hours before testing the meat. When the meat is tender – don't cook it so long that it falls to pieces – take the pot from the oven.

To serve hot, follow the suggestions in the first paragraph. Alternatively, leave it to cool down for about 30 minutes. Then take out the meat and the trotters. Line a colander with muslin or a cloth, strain the sauce through it, then pour it into a bowl and transfer it to the refrigerator.

Take all the little pieces of salt pork and the carrots out of the colander and put them with the meat.

For serving the beef, when cool carve half of it into slices, not too thick, arrange them neatly in a shallow bowl or oval platter, surround the beef with the sliced carrots and the little pieces of salt pork. Keep the other half, covered, in the refrigerator.

Remove all fat from the top of the jellied sauce – there will be a great deal; it can be clarified and used for frying croûtons. Melt half the jelly by putting it in a bowl over simmering water. When just melted pour it over the meat and leave to set.

Altogether there should be enough meat and jelly to make two meals for six people. The result of the lengthy, slow cooking is perfectly tender meat, while the wine, brandy and salt pork have combined with the beef and pig's trotters to produce a richly aromatic and beautiful dark, clear jelly, much like the one in a *bœuf mode*, but richer and even better. The smell of an *estouffat albigeois* during cooking is something memorable.

→ Cold Baked Salt Silverside of Beef ←

Salt silverside of beef is a true English specialty often overlooked when it comes to entertaining. A pity, for it is delicious and, when served cold, is economical and presents the minimum of cooking and serving problems.

Give your butcher warning that you will be needing a handsome piece of salt beef, otherwise he may not have any which has been long enough in the pickle.

Before cooking the beef soak it in cold water for a couple of hours.

5–6lb of salt silverside of beef; carrots; onions; garlic; bay leaves; peppercorns. Optional: a tumbler of cider or red wine.

Put the beef in a deep ovenproof pot in which there is not too much room to spare. Surround it with a couple of large carrots and onions sliced, a crushed clove of garlic, 2 bay leaves, half a dozen peppercorns and, if you are using it, the cider or wine – all these extra flavorings not only improve the taste of the meat but help to produce a stock that will make the basis of a beautiful beetroot or onion soup. Fill up the pot with water. Cover the pot closely.

Place in a very moderate oven, 325°F, and leave untouched

for 3–4 hours. Test to see if the meat is tender. Don't let it overcook, or it will crumble when carved. Take the joint from the liquid, wrap it in greaseproof paper, put it in a deep bowl. On top of it put a teaplate or small board, and a 2lb weight. Leave until the next day. With the beef have a green salad, and perhaps a mild fruit pickle such as the tomato and orange mixture given in "Sauces, Pickles and Chutney."

⤜ Brisket of Beef in Jelly ⤛

At a cold lunch or supper party you obviously do not want all your meat to be salt. Fresh brisket, being fat and moist, provides an agreeable contrast. Here is a dish which comes out looking and tasting something like the French bœuf mode, except that it is less highly flavored and that brisket, being already well inter-larded with its own fat, does not require the studding with pork fat which is necessary for the drier cuts such as topside and top rump which are usually chosen for the French dish.

Ingredients are 5–6lb of fresh brisket, boned, rolled and tied; 3 tablespoons of beef or pork lard, 2 pig's feet; ½ a bottle of sweetish white wine; 1–1¼ pints of water; 3 or 4 sprigs of parsley, a couple of bay leaves and a sprig or two of thyme tied into a little bunch; a crushed clove of garlic; salt.

To cook the beef, choose a heavy iron or earthenware pot in which the meat will fit with just enough room to spare for the pig's feet and the liquid. Heat the fat and let the meat just gently take color all round. Add the split pig's feet. Pour in the wine and the water and add the bunch of herbs, the gar-

lic and a dessertspoon of salt. The liquid should reach just
about level with the meat. Cover the pot with foil or greaseproof paper and the lid. Transfer it to a very moderate oven,
325°F, and let it cook for about 5 hours.

Take out the meat, strain the liquid into a bowl. Leave it
until next day to set. Take off the fat. There will be a beautiful brown jelly underneath. When you have carved the meat
and arranged it on a big round flat dish, chop up the jelly and
put it in a mound in the center.

This is an adapted version of a dish called *Beef à la Royal*
which is given by W. A. Henderson in his *Housekeeper's Instruc-
tor or Universal Family Cook*, published about 1800. In his recipe
the brisket is studded with parsley, little pieces of bacon and
oysters – a method of introducing salt into the meat. The
wine specified was sack or Madeira, which in the past were
used in considerable quantities in English cookery.

⤳ ROLLED AND GLAZED OX-TONGUE ⤴
*Ask your butcher for a brined ox-tongue, and whatever he may
instruct you to the contrary, soak it for a minimum of 12–18 hours
prior to cooking, in a big basin of cold water changed at least once.*

Rinse the tongue, put it in a large pan and cover it copiously
with cold water. In this case there is not much point in putting vegetables with the tongue; they will make no difference
to its taste, and the cooking liquid is usually too salty to use
for stock.

Bring the water very slowly to simmering point. Skim
several times, then cover the pot and simmer steadily but not
too fast for about 3½ hours for a tongue weighing approximately 5lb.

While the tongue is still hot, remove all the little bones,
trim off the gristly bits at the root end, and peel off the skin.

This has to be done very carefully in order not to damage the tongue itself.

Curl the tongue round in a cake tin in which it will just fit. (A tin with a removable base makes the eventual turning out of the tongue much easier.) Press it down. On top put a plate that should preferably fit just inside the tin. Weight it well and leave until the next day.

When you turn it out you can, if you happen to have some meat glaze or jelly from another dish, glaze the tongue. To do this put about a quarter of a cupful in a small pot in a bain-marie, let it melt, and when it has cooled again, but before it sets, paint the tongue with a pastry brush dipped in the jelly. Repeat this three or four times, as each coating sets. Failing home-made meat glaze or jelly, few people nowadays would have any hesitation about using packet aspic.

A smoked ox-tongue is drier, harder and more compact than a straightforward brined one. It will need 48 hours steeping in cold water, changed at least twice. Bring it, very slowly, to simmering point and thereafter allow one hour to each 1lb. The average weight of a smoked tongue is 3–3½lb. It is cooked when a skewer will pierce the thickest part quite easily.

✦ SUCKLING PIG ROASTED IN THE OVEN ✦

In the old days, of course, suckling pigs were roasted on the spit but it is a very easy animal to cook in the oven. However, as almost the most important part of it is considered to be the crackling, it should be eaten hot, for although the rich meat is delicious cold, the crackling goes tough and leathery as it cools.

For the stuffing for a suckling pig weighing in the region of 10–12lb, mix together ½lb of fine dry bread crumbs, a big bunch of parsley (about 2oz) finely chopped with 2 or 3 shallots and a clove or two of garlic; add the grated peel of a whole large lemon and of an orange; add the juices of both. Mix in 6oz of softened butter, about a teaspoon of salt, plenty of freshly milled pepper and a little grated nutmeg. Finally stir in 3 whole eggs, well beaten. Taste to see if there is sufficient lemon, for suckling pig is a rich meat and the stuffing for it should provide a mildly acid contrast; for this reason sausage meat, chestnuts, prunes and other such rather cloying ingredients are not so suitable for stuffings as the simple herb and lemon mixture.

Having stuffed the pig, give it a generous coating of olive oil, and if possible cook it on a rack in the baking dish so that the underside does not stew in its own juices. Put it in a moderate, preheated oven, 350°F, for 2–2½ hours altogether. From time to time baste it with its own juices, or with more olive oil. When it is ready to serve, transfer it to a hot dish and keep it in a low oven while you pour off from the baking tin as much as possible of the fat, transferring the gravy to a small pan. To this add a little glass of white wine and, if you have it, an equal quantity of clear veal or beef stock. Give it a quick boil and serve it separately.

To serve the piglet, cut off the head, and then split the animal completely in two. To carve, the shoulder and leg are separated from the carcass on one side, then the ribs cut into two or three helpings; these, with the neck-end between the shoulders, are traditionally considered to be the finest morsels. The ears, separated from the head, were also once regarded as special delicacies.

In old English cookery the brains were scooped out from the head and mixed with the gravy from the pig, some of the stuffing, and plenty of melted butter, to make a sauce. Nowadays if extra sauce is needed, most people would probably prefer an apple sauce or redcurrant jelly.

Many modern domestic ovens are too small to take a

whole suckling pig, although the length of the animal depends, of course, upon the breed of the pig. Should it be found that the piglet has to be cooked in two pieces, the best plan is to get the butcher to cut off the head and neck, which can either be roasted at the same time as the back and hindquarters or kept for a separate dish. (It makes a galantine of great finesse; some young children to whom I gave a galantine of suckling pig thought it was chicken, than which, from the nursery, there is no higher praise.) If this plan is followed, two-thirds of the amount of stuffing will be enough.

→ BAKED SALT PORK WITH A SALAD OF ORANGES ←
A hand of salted or pickled pork corresponds to the forehock in bacon. It is a cheap and easy joint to cook for a small household and makes a good alternative to a ham. Most good butchers will put one in brine for you if you give 4 or 5 days' notice. Get him also to bone and roll the joint.

The prepared joint will weigh approximately 6lb. Soak it for 6–12 hours, then put it in a deep baking tin or earthenware pot with a couple of onions and carrots, and water just to cover. Cover the pot, cook in a moderate oven, 325°F, for 3 hours. If the pan is not big enough for the joint to be quite covered with water, turn it over at half-time.

When cooked, leave to cool in its liquid for about an hour, then transfer it to a bowl, put a piece of greaseproof paper over it, and a plate or board with a weight on top. Leave until next day before cutting. There is no necessity to remove the rind – not being smoked it is soft and perfectly easy to carve through. The cooking liquid makes the basis of an excellent beetroot consommé or thick lentil or split pea soup.

A similar-sized piece of leg of pickled pork, which is a

leaner and more expensive cut, can be cooked in just the same way.

To go with the pork have a bowl of orange salad made from small, thin-skinned oranges, unpeeled, sliced into very thin rounds and with pips removed. Dress the oranges with a little sugar, wine vinegar and port, and sprinkle with dried mint. This is all the better for being made a day in advance.

Alternatively, the best of all sauces to go with gammon and pickled pork is Cumberland sauce (see "Sauces, Pickles and Chutney").

✥ Boned Baked Gammon ✥

The advantages of a boned and tied gammon over one on the bone are much greater ease in handling, cooking and storing. The flavor and cutting qualities in no way suffer from the boning, and I think the only criticism one might make is that the imposing appearance of a joint on the bone is lost. But in a household where cooking and storage facilities are limited, something has to be sacrificed. Also, the flavor of all cured meats slow-cooked in the oven without water is immeasurably superior to that of all boiled ones.

For a baked gammon of about 11lb, a minimum of 36 hours' preliminary soaking is essential – and 48 would be preferable, since the meat will have no further contact with any water or other liquid whatsoever. Also the water should be changed twice during the steeping. It is at this point that one already begins to appreciate the advantages of a boned gammon. Instead of the cumbersome ham kettle or outside crock required for the soaking of a ham or gammon on the bone, a large light plastic bowl kept especially for such purposes eliminates much of the preliminary heaving and carrying.

When the gammon is ready to cook, wrap it in two separate sheets of cooking foil – if you can get the extra wide size so much the better – and arrange these so that the joins come one on each side of the gammon. Stand the parcel on a rack placed in a baking tin. Fill the tin with water. Place low down in the oven, heated to very moderate, 325°F, and cook for just 5 hours, simply turning the parcel over at half-time.

Remove the parcel from the oven but do not unwrap it until the gammon has cooled quite considerably – at least for an hour. Then carefully strip off the skin, without removing the strings. (If the gammon is left until it is quite cold, as so often instructed, the skinning operation becomes very difficult.) Press home-made golden bread crumbs on to the exposed surface. Wrap up again and leave until next day. Then wrap in clean greaseproof paper, renewed every couple of days as you cut the gammon.

I don't advise sugar-glazing a gammon cooked in this way. A shiny toffee-brown coating may look very festive, but the second baking process involved tends to dry and toughen the outside of the joint.

All the liquid and fat which runs from the gammon when you unwrap it, as well as that in the tin, should be poured into a bowl and left until the fat has set and you can take it off. The liquid will be a bit salty, but can be used, diluted, as stock for a lentil or dried-pea soup.

A smaller joint of gammon, say a 5–6lb cut from the middle or corner, is cooked in precisely the same way, allowing a minimum of 24 hours' soaking, and for the baking 30 minutes per 1lb at the temperature as given for the whole gammon.

✻ Christmas in France ✻

*Dinner on Christmas Eve in a French farmhouse of the pre-1914 era
was a succession of homely country dishes for which almost every ingredient would have been produced on the farm itself. A characteristic
menu, sustaining and solid, reads as follows:*

Poule au riz à la fermière

Jambon cuit au foin

Petits pois jaunes en purée

Dindonneaux farcis aux marrons

Salade de céleris et betteraves

Poires étuvées au vin rouge

Galettes à la boulangère

Fromage de la ferme

Café. Vieux Marc

Vins: Moulin-à-Vent et . . . eau du puits

*Escoffier, recording the dinner in a professional culinary magazine in
the year 1912, thought it, in its "rustic simplicity," worthy of inclusion
among the festive menus of the Majestics, the Palaces, the Ritz-Carl-
tons, the Excelsiors of Europe. How many of these menus, he asks,
would be in such perfect taste? One senses a hint of envy in his words,
for any chef who served such a menu in an English restaurant of the
period would have been a laughing-stock. At the Carlton (where
Escoffier was then presiding) the Christmas menu for that year started
with the inevitable caviar and turtle soup, and went on through the fillets of sole with crayfish sauce, the quails and stuffed lettuces, lamb
cutlets, out of season asparagus, the foie gras and frosted tangerines,
to start again with the truffled turkey, celery salad, plum pudding,
hothouse peaches, friandises. At one elegant Paris restaurant, the Mar-
guery, the 1913 Christmas Eve dinner consisted of one service only:*

Elizabeth David's Christmas

Huîtres natives
Consommé chaud aux œufs pochés
Timbale de Homard Américaine
Poularde et faisan truffés
Salade de saison
Pâté de foie gras à la gelée
Glace Cendrillon
Plum-pudding, Bûche de Noël
Desserts

Oysters, consommé with poached eggs, timbale of lobster, truffled chicken and pheasant, green salad, pâté de foie gras (in those days served after the roast rather than as an hors-d'œuvre), an ice, plum pudding or bûche de Noël, fruit. The only concession to the festive season is the inclusion of the plum pudding and Yule log, otherwise it might have been a well-chosen dinner for any winter's evening. For Christmas in France has never been quite the occasion for the prodigious feasts of the Germanic and Anglo-Saxon countries. A people for whom food is one of the first considerations every day of the year tend to regard the English preoccupation with eating for one week only out of the fifty-two as rather gross.

Alfred Suzanne, whose book on La Cuisine Anglaise (he had been chef to the Duke of Bedford and the Earl of Wilton) is still the chief source of information to the French about English cooking, referred to the "hecatombs of turkeys, geese, game of all sorts, the holocaust of fatted oxen, pigs and sheep . . . mountains of plum puddings, ovens full of mince-pies." Philéas Gilbert, another well-known contemporary chef, went to some trouble to prove that "le plum pudding n'est pas anglais," but graciously conceded that, being already so rich in national dishes, the French could easily afford to leave the English in possession of their supposedly national Christmas pudding.

In most French country households the réveillon supper, however elegant the rest of the food, includes ritual dishes of humble origin such as boudins or blood puddings in some form or other, and various kinds of bread, biscuits, and galettes to which some ancient religious significance is attached. In Provence no fewer than thirteen of these desserts are traditional, while the main course is always a fish dish, usually salt cod, accompanied by snails, potatoes and other vegetables, salads and big bowls of the shining golden aïoli for which the finest olive oil has been reserved. For here the Christmas Eve supper is eaten before the celebration of Midnight Mass, and is therefore a maigre meal, shared by all the family, attended by the ceremony of sprinkling the Yule log with wine before setting it upon the fire, and the pronouncement, by the master of the house, of the ritual prayer "May God grant us grace to see the next year, and if there should not be more of us, let there not be fewer."

When, as in Gascony and parts of the Languedoc, the great Christmas dish is one of those beef and wine estouffats which has been giving out its aromatic scents from the hearth where it has been simmering all day long, it will probably be eaten at one o'clock in the morning after the family comes back from Mass. The recipe for one such dish, from the Albi district, is so beautifully simple that its possibilities during the days of busy preparations for the festivities will be readily appreciated. For the rest, French turkeys, geese, hams and chickens are cooked much like our own, although the stuffings may vary, and the accompaniments are very much simpler – potatoes and a salad, a purée of dried split peas or a dish of rice, rather than the sprouts, the peas, the bread sauces, the gravies and sweet jellies of the English Christmas table.

Vegetables

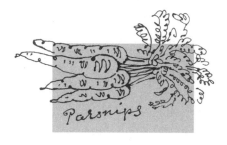

Parsnips

≈≈≈ · **VII** · ≋≋≋

URING THE pre-Christmas period fresh vegetables tend to become so expensive that large numbers of families depend on the freezer – their own or the one in the nearest supermarket – for supplies over the long holiday. Reasonably enough. Who wants to stand over the sink cleaning pounds of Brussels sprouts and scrubbing colanders full of carrots when there is so much other work to be done?

The great Christmas meal over, however, a craving for a few vegetables freshly and simply cooked soon sets in, and a meal made up entirely of vegetables and fruit, or eggs and salads, without so much as a sniff of the turkey or ham leftovers begins to seem enormously desirable. So in this book I am suggesting a few easily prepared and quickly cooked vegetable dishes for the days before and after Christmas. Most of them are ideas and reminders rather more than formally articulated recipes.

It is easy to devise delicious and unusual combinations of vegetables, but in the exhaustion of Christmas entertaining it is equally easy to forget the good ideas you had during the rest of the year and fall back on the routine potatoes, cabbage, sprouts.

Celery and Belgian Endives Most useful standby vegetables for the Christmas period. Raw and in salads they taste clean and fresh. For flavoring soups and stews and poultry leftovers celery leaves are capital. For quick vegetable dishes both celery and endives can be sliced and sautéed in butter. Endives baked with butter in a covered pan in a low oven for 1–1½ hours are refreshing and astringent. An endive and potato purée, enriched with milk or cream and flavored with Parmesan, has a friendly bitter-soft quality. A strong, clear chicken or beef consommé flavored with celery, then thickened with egg yolk and lemon, is delicate and restorative.

Cress Why is it that cress – of the mustard and cress kind – so rarely figures in our cooking? In soups I find it makes a welcome change from watercress – quite often difficult to get hold of in the winter – and is also an interesting alternative to parsley in salads, all manner of omelettes, fish dishes and sauces. Since it keeps well in its little punnets – for that matter it is child's play, literally, to grow it – it makes a valuable stand-by when other fresh green herbs are lacking. I have included it in several recipes in this book, notably the parsnip recipe in "Soups" and as an alternative to parsley in the celery and mushroom dish below.

↦ MARINATED CARROTS ↤
An old favorite, particularly useful during the Christmas season.

For 2lb of young or youngish carrots, prepare a marinade of ⅓ pint each of wine vinegar, white wine or cider, and water, plus 1 teaspoon each of salt and sugar, a few parsley stalks, a branch of dried thyme and a couple of bay leaves tied in a bunch, a small clove of garlic crushed, and 4fl oz of olive oil. Dijon mustard is needed when the carrots are cooked.

Scrub the carrots – don't peel them if you can avoid it – and slice them into quarters lengthwise. Bring the marinade to the boil, throw in the carrots, let them boil fairly fast until they are just cooked but not too soft. With a slotted spoon transfer them from the marinade to a serving dish.

Remove the bunch of herbs from the marinade. While it is still hot stir in a tablespoon of Dijon mustard. Taste for seasoning and pour the marinade back over the carrots. Leave to cool.

Excellent with cold duck or goose, and also with a terrine of pork, and as part of a cold first course of mixed vegetable dishes.

✣ Leeks with Red Wine ✤
Unexpectedly, perhaps, when wine is to be used in the cooking of leeks, the French always use red rather than white wine.

Choose small leeks, all of a size. Having cut them down almost to the white part and cleaned them thoroughly, put them side by side in a frying-pan in which you have heated 3 or 4 tablespoons of olive oil. As soon as they have taken color on one side, turn them over. Season with very little salt. Pour over them, for 1lb of leeks, a wineglass of red wine (look out for the spluttering), let it bubble, add 2 tablespoons of good meat stock, or water if no stock is available, cover the pan and cook at a moderate pace for 7–10 minutes, turning the leeks over once during the process. They are done when a skewer pierces the root end quite easily. Put the leeks on a shallow oval dish, cook the sauce another few seconds until reduced and pour it over the leeks. Serve hot as a separate vegetable course, or cold as an hors-d'œuvre.

✦ Sweet-Sour Cabbage ✦

For this you need a large wide sauté pan, or an old-fashioned
deep fryer, more or less in the shape of a Chinese wok.
The recipe, however, is an Italian one.

Ingredients are: a good hard little white cabbage weighing about 2lb, or half a larger one, olive oil, salt, sugar, wine vinegar, parsley.

Cut out and discard the hard stalk part from the cabbage. Slice the rest into thin ribbons. Heat 2 or 3 tablespoons of olive oil in the pan. Throw in the cabbage before the oil gets too hot. Sauté it quickly, turning it over and over with a wooden spatula. Add salt, say 2 teaspoons, but you have to taste. Cover the pan. Leave it for 5 minutes. Uncover it, stir, and turn again, adding 2 level tablespoons of sugar and 2 of wine vinegar. Cover and leave another 5 minutes. Taste for the seasoning. Turn into a wide shallow serving dish or salad bowl. Strew with chopped parsley. This is good as a vegetable dish on its own. Or serve it as a salad with ham or cold roast pork.

✦ Variation: Sweet-Sour Cabbage ✦
with Spiced Prunes

Cook the cabbage as in the recipe above. During the final minutes of cooking add 8 or 10 spiced prunes prepared as in the recipe given in the "Desserts" chapter. A beautiful dish.

But take great care that the cabbage is still a little bit crisp and that the prunes retain their identity.

A little grated lemon peel mixed in with the chopped parsley before it is strewn over the cabbage adds an agreeable tang.

✦ CREAM OF PARSNIPS WITH GINGER AND EGGS ✦

Boil 1lb scrubbed parsnips in their skins, as for the Pastenak and Cress Cream (see "Soups"). Drain, purée them in the blender. Season the purée with a little grated ginger root, salt and freshly milled pepper. Thin with a little of the reserved cooking water and a spoonful or two of olive oil. Spoon into three individual egg dishes. On top of each put a halved hard-boiled egg, cut side downward. Strew with bread crumbs and a little more olive oil. Cook in a medium-hot oven, 350°F, for about 10 minutes until the purée is hot and the bread crumbs golden brown.

✦ CELERY AND MUSHROOMS ✦
A fresh and quickly cooked little vegetable dish.

You need olive oil, walnut oil or sesame oil for frying; a large head of celery – washed, trimmed, and cut in slantwise slices about 2 inches long; salt; ¼lb of mushrooms – briefly rinsed, dried, and sliced, stalks and all; a scrap of crushed garlic; freshly milled pepper; parsley or cress.

Warm just enough oil to spread over the base of a 10-inch frying or sauté pan. Put in the prepared celery. Add salt. Sauté for 5 minutes. Add the mushrooms and the crushed garlic. Cook for another 3 or 4 minutes. Grind in a little black pepper. Strew with chopped parsley or cress and serve hot. Enough for three, and good with almost anything as well as on its own.

⇥ CHESTNUTS WITH BACON ⇤

Score the chestnuts across on the round side and toast them in a low oven, 325°F, for 15 minutes until both shell and skin can be peeled off. For 2lb of chestnuts put ¼lb of bacon cut in pieces into a casserole, add the chestnuts and water to cover. Cook for about 30 minutes. Serve with turkey, roast hare, or as a separate dish.

Brussels Sprouts

"Was it T. H. Huxley who commented during the Darwinian contro-versy that even the Archbishop of Canterbury consists of 90% water? This is certainly true of Brussels sprouts and those irrigated during the parched autumn (of 1978) are among the finest for Christmas gour-mandising. . . ."

TONY VENISON
"Flavors of Christmas"
Country Life, 21 December 1978

I don't presume to tell readers how to cook Brussels sprouts, except just to put in a plea for undercooking rather than the reverse. Try steaming them.

A few roughly broken up cooked chestnuts mixed in with the sprouts just before they are ready makes an understand-ably well-loved combination.

Somewhere recently I saw a recipe for a soup made with Brussels sprouts. It was flavored with leeks and grapefruit juice, and sounded very unengaging indeed. For a gardening writer's notion – a good one I think – of a sprout salad, see Sprouts in a Green Salad in "Winter Salads."

→ JERUSALEM ARTICHOKES WITH ←
TOMATOES AND HERBS

Simmer your artichokes in salted water until they are almost, but not quite, cooked. Strain them. Cut each in two. Heat a little olive oil in a heavy pan, put in the artichokes and, for each 1lb, add 2 skinned and chopped tomatoes, and a seasoning of dried basil or marjoram chopped with a little scrap of garlic, salt and freshly milled pepper. By the time the tomatoes have melted to form a sauce, the artichokes should be quite tender and the dish ready to serve, either by itself or as an accompaniment to lamb, pork or sausages. This is a dish that also goes remarkably well with goose.

→ JERUSALEM ARTICHOKES WITH CREAM ←

Choose large artichokes for this dish, allowing ½lb per person, and, having peeled them, slice them thinly and as evenly as possible. In a thick frying-pan, melt a little butter, put in the artichokes, rinsed and drained, and let them absorb the butter. Season, just cover with water, and cook steadily in the open pan until nearly all the liquid is evaporated and the artichokes are tender. For 1lb of artichokes pour in 3 tablespoons of cream, a scrap of nutmeg, some chopped parsley, cook another minute and squeeze in a few drops of lemon.

→ PUMPKIN AND TOMATO GRATIN ←

A 2lb piece of pumpkin, 1lb tomatoes, 2 sticks of celery or the tops of a whole small head, 1½oz butter, salt, garlic if you like, parsley, about 4 tablespoons of coarse bread crumbs.

Peel the pumpkin, discard the seeds and the cottony center core; cut into small chunks. Skin and chop the tomatoes. Wash and chop the celery.

In a large heavy frying-pan heat 1oz of the butter, put in the celery, the pumpkin, and 1 scant tablespoon of salt. Cook gently, uncovered, until the pumpkin is soft and just beginning to look slightly jammy. Transfer it to a shallow gratin dish. In the same pan cook the tomatoes, with the garlic if you are using it, a little more salt and some chopped parsley. When most of the moisture has evaporated and the tomatoes are almost in a purée, mix with the pumpkin, smooth down the top (the dish should be quite full), cover with the bread crumbs and the remaining butter cut into tiny knobs, stand the dish on a baking sheet and cook near the top of a fairly hot oven, 350°F, for 35–40 minutes, until the top surface is golden and crisp.

⤙ BAKED STUFFED TOMATOES À LA GRECQUE ⤙

2 large tomatoes for each person. For a dozen tomatoes: ¼lb of rice, boiled and drained, a small onion, butter, 2oz of currants soaked in warm water, salt, pepper, nutmeg, chopped parsley, a teaspoon of dried mint, olive oil.

Halve the tomatoes, scoop out the flesh, add it to the rice. Fry the chopped onion pale golden in a little butter. Mix with the rice, which should be very well seasoned. Add the drained currants, seasoning of salt, pepper and nutmeg, a good deal of chopped parsley and a teaspoonful or so of dried mint. Pile this rice stuffing into the tomatoes. Pour a little olive oil on top of each half tomato (it is important that the rice should remain moist, and not emerge from the oven with a hard crust on the top). Put them in an oiled baking dish and bake at 325°F for 45 minutes to an hour.

Should your oven be too cramped for the tomatoes to bake on the top shelf, then you have to resort to the following device: into your largest frying-pan pour 3 tablespoonfuls of olive oil, put in as many of the stuffed halved tomatoes as it will take. Fry these very gently for a few minutes, until they start to soften. Transfer them to a baking tin or large gratin dish. Repeat the process with the rest of the tomatoes. Finish cooking them under the grill, but as far away from the heat and as slowly as possible, to avoid burning the rice. (A few bread crumbs strewn over the top of each and moistened with olive oil make a protective layer between the rice and the heat.)

✦ Sweet-Sour Red Cabbage and Sausages ✦
This dish is one for the large kitchen, for you need plenty of elbow room for the preparation. You also need either one very large deep enameled cast-iron, glazed earthenware or other oven pot, or two smaller ones in which two-thirds of the cooking can be done and then when the cabbage has diminished in volume all can be transferred into one pot.

2 average-sized red cabbages, 4 large Bramley apples, 2 large onions, 4 tablespoons of brown sugar, 2 teaspoons of ground allspice; salt and freshly milled pepper; a bouquet of bay leaves, thyme sprigs, a stick of celery and a piece of orange peel tied together, 6–7 tablespoons of wine vinegar or cider vinegar, 2–3lb of Strasbourg, Frankfurt or similar smoked sausages.

Remove the outer leaves of the cabbages and set them aside. Cut each cabbage in quarters and slice them as thin as you can, discarding the hard white center and stalks. Peel and slice the apples and onions. Pack the cabbage, onions and apples in layers, sprinkling each with the sugar and seasonings as you go. Right in the center put the bouquet (if you are doing the cooking in two pots, make two bouquets). Pour over the vinegar. Over the top arrange the reserved outer leaves of the cabbage, which will prevent the top layer from drying up. Cover also with a piece of paper and a close-fitting lid. Cook in a very low oven, 300°F, for a minimum of 4 hours. By this time the cabbage will have shrunk to manageable proportions and there will be room to put the sausages in the center and to repack the rest of the ingredients on the top, covering once more with the outer leaves and lid. Cook for at least another hour.

These quantities should serve about ten people. This is an expandable dish and just about indestructible however long it is left to cook or however many times it is reheated.

The dish can be supplemented with baked or grilled gammon rashers, and a creamy sauce, uncooked, to be made as follows: Sieve 7–8oz of fresh cream cheese, stir in ¼ pint of single cream, a little very finely chopped onion or shallot, parsley, fresh mint when you can get it, freshly milled pepper, salt. This sauce served cold makes a delicious contrast with the sweet-and-sour cabbage and the sausages.

⊀ VARIATION: RED CABBAGE ⊁
AS AN ACCOMPANIMENT

Half the quantity of cabbage, apple, onion and flavorings cooked for 3 hours is enough for 4–6 as an accompanying vegetable. It goes well with goose and pork. The cabbage can be cooked a day in advance, as it improves, if anything, with reheating.

✳ An Eighteenth-Century Kitchen Garden ✳ at Christmas

An interesting little book called The Complete English Gardener by Samuel Cooke, undated but published simultaneously and in the same volume with Mrs. Alice Smith's Art of Cookery (1760), gives us a good picture of fruit and vegetables both hothouse and outdoor, grown for the Christmas season in an English country-house garden of the period. This is no imaginary or theoretical list, for Samuel Cooke, we learn from the title page of the book, was gardener at Overton in Wiltshire, and had "practised gardening, thro' all its branches, in many countries, upwards of Forty years." The frontispiece shows a handsome Georgian manor house. Opening his "work of the month" dissertation with the sardonic comment that "a very principal part of the business of the month consists in its being esteemed a greater excellency to produce a single cucumber or cherry at Christmass, than to bring to maturity loads of them in their natural season," Cooke goes on to say that with the help of a forcing frame "We may have some green peas in December and January," goes into detail about the way to bring cherries in December – he doesn't promise success in this dicey enterprise – and finally gives the following list.

PRODUCE OF THE MONTH

We have in the conservatory some artichoaks preserved in the sand. There are several sorts of cabbages, and their sprouts, for boiling; asparagus upon hot-beds; and if diligence has been used, you may find some cucumbers, of the plants which were sown in July and August.

We have this month on the hot-bed sallads of small herbs, with mint, terragon, burnet, cabbage-lettuce preserved under glasses, and some cresses and chervil upon the natural ground, with which high taste helps the sallads of this season. To these may be added blanched celery and endive.

There are variety of herbs for soups and the kitchen use, such as sage, thyme, beet-leaves, parsley, sorrel, spinach, cellery, and leeks, tops of young peas etc. Likewise sweet marjoram, dried marygold flowers, and dried mint. The roots are carrots, parsnips, turneps, and potatoes.

The fruit garden produces little this month, except pears and apples; of the latter we have but few, tho' there are yet plenty of the former, particularly of the St Germain, ambret, and the col-mar.

The flowers we have this month are single anemones, stock-gilliflowers, single wall-flowers, primroses, snowdrops, black hellebore, winter aconite, polyanthus; and in the hot-beds the narcissus and the hyacinth.

The Complete English Gardener, SAMUEL COOKE,
Gardener at Overton, in Wiltshire.
London: Printed for J. Cooke,
at Shakespear's-Head,
in Pater-noster-Row.
(Price 1s. 6d)

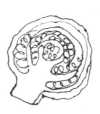

Winter Salads

AT MIDDAY, my winter salads often take the form of a very simple little hors-d'œuvre such as a bowl of freshly grated carrots, shredded celeriac, or a raw cabbage and sweet pepper salad with a rather sharp dressing flavored with crushed juniper berries.

✣ CAROTTES RAPÉES ✦

Grate 6–8 medium-sized cleaned raw carrots coarsely. When the hard yellow core of the carrots is reached, discard it. To the grated carrots add 1 small grated shallot (you get more or less only the juice by grating a shallot, which is correct), a teaspoon of salt, the juice of a quarter of a lemon, a pinch of sugar, 3 tablespoons of olive oil and a dash of vinegar.

Serve on a small shallow dish as part of a mixed hors-d'œuvre. This refreshing and brightly colored little salad is especially welcome when other ingredients of the hors-d'œuvre are rather fat, like a salad of pig's cheek, or rich, like an egg mayonnaise.

✣ CÉLERI-RAVE RÉMOULADE ✦

To make this celeriac hors-d'œuvre – a dish familiar to anyone who has eaten regularly in the smaller restaurants of

Paris and the French provinces – you do really need to be in possession of that invaluable utensil known as a mandoline. On the fluted blade of the mandoline shred the peeled celeriac into matchstick pieces (or use a julienne blade in a food processor. JN). As you proceed, put all into a bowl of cold water acidulated with lemon juice or vinegar. Bring a big saucepan of water, also acidulated, and salted, to the boil. Plunge the drained celeriac into it. Leave it until the water comes back to the boil again, no longer; then drain it as dry as you can, in a colander. This brief blanching makes all the difference to a celeriac salad, for in its totally raw state many people find it hard to digest. Also, after blanching, it absorbs less dressing or mayonnaise.

When the celeriac has cooled, mix it with a very stiff home-made mayonnaise very strongly flavored with mustard. Pile the celeriac on to a shallow dish, sprinkle it with parsley, and serve it fairly quickly; if left to stand for any length of time it begins to look rather unattractive and messy.

An average-sized celeriac, weighing approximately 1lb, plus about ⅓ pint of mayonnaise (2 egg yolks) will make an ample hors-d'œuvre for four.

⤳ Endive and Beetroot Salad ⤶

1lb of Belgian endives or chicory, olive oil, salt, freshly milled pepper, lemon juice, 2 medium-sized cooked beetroots, tarragon vinegar.

Discard the outside leaves of the endives; cut off the root ends, using a stainless steel or silver knife; wipe the endives clean with a soft cloth. Cut them across into ½ inch chunks. Put the prepared endives in a bowl. Mix them with a dressing of olive oil, salt, freshly milled pepper and lemon juice.

Prepare the beetroots separately. Peel them, dice them,

season with plenty of salt, freshly milled pepper and a dressing of oil and a very little tarragon vinegar. At the last moment, put the beetroot in the salad bowl in the center of the endives.

✣ CELERY AND BEETROOT SALAD ✣

An admirable winter salad to serve either after a chicken or meat dish or at Christmas with your turkey. The peeled and diced beetroot is dressed with a highly seasoned oil and vinegar dressing, a scrap of garlic, chopped parsley. The celery, cut into julienne strips, is separately seasoned with oil, salt and lemon, and piled lightly on top of the beetroot just before serving.

✣ SPROUTS IN A GREEN SALAD ✣

Brussels sprout entries at vegetable shows are among the few in which judges regard obesity as a fault, the small, tight-buttoned Noisette frequently scooping most prizes. . . "Shelled" and grated raw, possibly with Parmesan cheese, sprouts provide seasonable green salading along with endive and chicory.

TONY VENISON, "Flavors of Christmas"
Country Life, 21 December 1978

✣ ORANGE SALAD ✣

Peel a few oranges and cut them in large pieces, taking out the pips, adding a few spoonfuls of orange-flower water, stir, then sprinkle lightly with powdered cinnamon. Is very soothing.

❧ Salad of Cos Lettuce ❧

A fine cos lettuce, finely chopped, sprinkled with the juice of 2 oranges, a pinch of salt and a good deal of pepper. A curious and very refreshing mixture.

❧ Angevin Salad ❧

This is a lovely salad to serve after a roast turkey or capon.

Hearts of 2 lettuces or of 2 curly endives or Batavian endives, ½lb of Gruyère or Emmenthal cheese, olive oil and wine vinegar for the dressing.

Salad and cheese in one course – not American but French, and very delicate and unusual. The salad must be fresh and crisp. Wash and dry it well ahead of time. With it in the bowl mix the Gruyère or Emmenthal (the latter is the one with the large holes, whereas the real Gruyère has very small ones) cut into tiny cubes. Add the dressing, made from 6 tablespoonfuls of olive oil to a teaspoonful or two at most of vinegar, at the last minute.

Instead of olive oil, the light walnut oil of Touraine can be used for the dressing. Combined with the cheese it makes a beautiful and interesting mixture.

❧ Leeks à la Provençale ❧

3lb of leeks, 2 tablespoons of olive oil, ½lb of tomatoes, 1 dozen black olives, juice of 1 lemon, 1 dessertspoon of finely chopped lemon peel.

Chop the cleaned leeks into ½ inch lengths. Into a shallow heatproof dish put the oil and when it is warm, but not smoking, put in the leeks, add a little salt and pepper, cover the pan and simmer for 10 minutes. Add the tomatoes cut in halves, the stoned olives, the lemon juice and the chopped lemon peel and cook slowly for another 10 minutes. Serve in the dish in which it has been cooked. This is excellent cold as a salad.

→ FENNEL SALAD ←

The raw fennel roots are washed and cut into small strips, dressed with oil and lemon juice, preferably 2 or 3 hours before serving.

→ ORANGE AND CELERY SALAD ←

Short pieces of celery and quarters of orange, with a very little dressing of oil and lemon. Especially good to accompany a terrine.

→ RICE AND CUCUMBER SALAD ←
This makes a good accompaniment to cold turkey and chicken.

For 6-8 people put 1lb of good-quality rice in a gallon-and-a-half capacity saucepan nearly full of boiling salted water. Add half a lemon and when the water comes back to the boil float a couple of tablespoons of oil on the top. This will help prevent the water boiling over. The rice will be cooked in 12-18 minutes depending on the type of rice you are using. In any case, keep it on the firm side.

As soon as you have drained the rice in a colander, turn it into a big bowl. Immediately, add any necessary salt, approximately 6 tablespoons of oil, 2 teaspoons of tarragon vinegar, 2 shallots sliced into paper-thin rounds, and a good quantity of grated nutmeg. This latter seasoning makes the whole difference.

Have ready a cucumber, peeled, sliced in four lengthways, the seeds removed, the flesh cut into small cubes, and seasoned with salt. Mix these with the rice. Add also, if you like, a dozen or so black olives, a few cubes of raw celery, and a few shreds of raw red or green pepper. Mix all together very lightly and the salad is ready, except for a sprinkling of chives or parsley.

As a change from cucumber, try instead little cubes of green or yellow honeydew melon, which goes well with both chicken and turkey.

✻ The Magpie System ✻

An organization we could do with at Christmas time is one which would provide packing depots — boutiques perhaps they would be called — places to which all one's miscellaneous presents could be taken, made up into seemly parcels and entrusted to the shop for postage or dispatch.

Parcel-wrapping stations in big stores are fine as far as they go but since one can hardly ask them to pack things bought in other shops, that isn't quite far enough. I was thinking particularly about hampers of food and wine. The roof under which one would be able to buy everything one would like to put into such parcels doesn't exist; my hampers would be based on a lot of small things; some cheap, some less so; they would be Christmas stockings really, not hampers, and one rule would be that everything should be the very best of its kind, and that means you have to go to specialist shops for coffee, three or four different kinds in labeled parcels (all ready-made hampers contain fine-quality tea, which is all very well for friends abroad, but silly in England; you can buy good tea anywhere; good coffee is infinitely more rare) which would include Mocha, Java, Blue Mountain. Then there would be little packets, neat and gaudy, of those spices which are not always easy to come by even in a city which not all that long ago was the center of the entire world spice trade.

The spice importing-exporting center appears to have moved to North America, and the English supermarketeers (and how sensible of them) have been quick to see the possibilities of American- and Canadian-packed whole spices, such as coriander seeds, allspice berries, cumin and fennel seeds, cinnamon sticks and ginger root. As a matter of fact, by buying one large packet of pickling spice you get, if you can identify them, a good selection of these spices (not the cumin or fennel seeds, though) which grocers are always denying they have in stock. For a phial of fine whole saffron — even I wouldn't need a professional packer for that — a well-found chemist is the best bet. Then, inevitably, an expedition to Soho and Roche of 14 Old Compton Street, the only shop selling the envelopes of herbs dried and packed on the stalk — wild thyme, basil, thick fennel twigs — that contain the right true essence of all the hills of Provence. And one could do worse than buy a gallon or two of their beautiful olive oil, and decant it into clear wine or liqueur bottles for presents.

Half the charm of the magpie system of shopping is that one comes across unexpectedly pretty and festive-looking things for so little money; in the window of the Empire Shop in Sloane Street there is a pyramid of white candy sugar in rocky lumps, so irresistibly decorative that one would like to hang them on the tree; and inside the shop, by-passing the chain-dairy goods which have somehow strayed in, are dark and dazzly genuine Indian chutneys, garnet-bright Jamaican guava jelly, English quince, Scottish rowan, and squat jars of shiny lemon curd.

Indeed, to think no further than how to make up hampers of jams and jellies, marmalade and honey would still be to have and to give plenty of entertainment.

Dark French heather honey from the Landes is one that I know to be especially aromatic, and there must be some fifty more different kinds of honey at least to be bought in London. Fortnum's seem to have the most dazzling choice; there can be found (if you dodge the gift packs, the china beehives, the peasant pottery) honey from Hungary and Guatemala, California and Canada and Dalmatia, from Buckfast and Jamaica, from Mexico, Sicily, Greece, Scotland, Italy, Ireland and Spain; and every aromatic flower of which one has ever heard has apparently fed those bees; lime flowers and rosemary, acacia, wild thyme, white clover, orange blossom and lemon and wild roses. With all their colors and different degrees of opacity or translucence, some creamy as white cornelian and some clear and golden as Château d'Yquem and some bronze as butterscotch, they have the allure that Christmas presents ought to have. Three Kings' presents perhaps. Just the quality that things in ready-made-up hampers hardly ever possess.

Those bottles of indeterminate sherry and port, Christmas puddings and tins of tea and fancy biscuits are survivals from the days when such things were distributed by Ladies Bountiful to old retainers, retired nannies and governesses and coachmen who would probably much rather have had a couple of bottles of gin. Well, wouldn't you? And really one would have to have quite a grievance against somebody before one felt impelled to give them a hamper – this is one from the list of a great West End store a year or two ago – containing one tin each of chicken, ox-tongue, steak, cocktail sausages, shrimps, ham, crab, dressed lobster and steak pie, plus one box of assorted cheese. Then there was the writer of a handout I once received from a public relations firm flogging Italian tomato products whose Christmas hamper idea was for two tins of tomato juice packed in a beribboned wicker basket, which would make, they ventured to suggest, a gift acceptable to "elderly people or neighbors." As Christmas approaches, people (and neighbors, too, I dare say) do tend to rather morbid ideas about others. But is that bad?

I'm not sure about the precise technical distinction between mushrooms and champignons, but Fortnum's hampers this year [1962] have come out in a rash of tinned champignon butter and champignon bisque; and here and there in the parcels directed at overseas customers are ready-made crêpes Suzette brought over from the United States; perhaps pancakes travel exceptionally well, and if they don't, they are, at any rate in Fortnumese, "Conversation Pieces of memorable quality." Harrods' man seems to have been bemused by dates in glove boxes and something called Bakon Krisp; Selfridges are bent on spreading the joyful tidings that you can buy shoestring potatoes in tins; Barkers' cheese hampers would be rather sensible, except that Prize Dairy Stilton and Assorted Cheese Portions seem to make such unlikely basket-fellows.

Inconsistency is characteristic of all Christmas hampers, but at least Christopher's, the wine merchants of 94 Jermyn Street, is one firm that has eliminated it from their Christmas lists this year. A case containing a bottle of manzanilla and two tins of Spanish green olives stuffed with anchovies makes sense; so does a bottle of Sercial Madeira and two large jars of turtle soup; and a bottle of champagne, plus a tin of foie gras for two, or a bottle of Club port and a jar of Stilton, are far more enterprising than the contents of most store-chosen hampers, and since Messrs Christopher's also sell first-pressing Provence olive oil and Barton and Guestier's fine white wine vinegar, it shouldn't be beyond the ingenuity of their directors to devise a salad-making or kitchen case which would be cheap and imaginative.

Sauces, Pickles, and Chutneys

· IX ·

SAUCES

✢ LEMON AND CELERY SAUCE ✦

This is a lovely sauce and very simple, although a bit extravagant, because unless you happen to be using the lemon peel for something else it is wasted. (See note below.)

FOR 3 PEOPLE you need 3 fat sticks of celery, 1 large lemon, 1½ tablespoons of sugar, 4 tablespoons of light olive oil, salt. Please note that by tablespoons I mean the present British standard measuring spoon which holds approximately ½oz. It is important to bear this in mind.

Clean, trim and chop the celery. Cut away all peel and every scrap of pith from the lemon. Cut the flesh into dice, discarding pips and central core. Put the lemon and sugar into a bowl standing in a saucepan over simmering water, or in the top half of a double saucepan, and let it cook until the sugar has melted. Add the chopped celery, olive oil and a little salt. Cook for 5 more minutes.

Good hot or cold, with chicken or turkey (in treble quantities) and also with fish. Not good for fine or delicate wine.

Note

One way of using the lemon peel would be to use a couple of strips to flavor an apple purée (see below). In that case, wash the lemon before paring it.

⇥ CELERY SAUCE ⇤

This is Cre-Fydd's recipe for the sauce to serve with Boned Turkey, Stuffed with Tongue and Forcemeat
(see "Poultry and Game").

Wash two heads of fine white celery, and cut it into small pieces; put it into a pint and a quarter of new milk, and simmer it until quite tender [about an hour] then rub it through a fine sieve; beat the yolks of four fresh eggs with a gill of thick cream; mix all together, and stir over a gentle fire for five or six minutes, till the sauce thickens, and serve as directed.

⇥ APPLE PURÉE OR SAUCE ⇤

To me, this is the one and only way to make a good apple purée or sauce that can be served with roast pork or goose. About twenty years ago I found the recipe in Eliza Acton's superb Modern Cookery *for Private Families, 1845, and with slight variations have been using it ever since. At one time I used apples from an old tree in my mother's garden at Enfield; we didn't know what variety those apples were, but they weren't at all like cookers as we know them today. They made superlative purée, light and clear pale green with no trace of that brownish, pasty look one often gets with modern Bramleys, due no doubt to the bruising to which Bramleys are so subject, although straight from the tree and just ripe they make very good cookers. After my mother sold the Enfield house I had to revert to bought Bramleys or whatever other cooking apple I could find. At Christmas time, in London at any rate, the only cookers available are Bramleys – which, incidentally, were evolved only during the second half of the nineteenth century, so would not have been known to Miss Acton.*

Say you have 4 or 5 large Bramleys – about 2lb – then the other ingredients, not very complicated, are 8 tablespoons (2 per apple) of water, about 4 of sugar, 1 of butter. Optionally, a strip of lemon peel. For cooking the apples, you need a very deep and capacious ovenproof pot, a big earthenware bowl or one of those large white ovenproof French soup tureens now often to be found in kitchen shops.

Core and peel the apples, discarding any bruised bits. With Bramleys there is often a good deal of waste, so if they look badly bruised, it's a good idea to allow one extra apple.

Slice the apples straight into the bowl, or pot, add the water and the lemon peel if you are using it. Cover the pot. This is important: if left uncovered the apples will discolor.

Put the pot on the center shelf of a moderate oven, 350°F. Leave for approximately 1 hour. Now have a look at the apples. They will probably still be a little underdone. Replace the lid and leave for another 10 or 15 minutes. By this time the apples should be quite soft and – when Bramleys are used – almost disintegrated. Take them out of the oven, beat them to a light purée, using a whisk. The sauce or purée is ready. Only now add the sugar and butter.

Note

Sometimes, if making the purée just for myself, I leave out both sugar and butter. At one time it seems to have been customary to add mustard to apple sauce. One recipe I have, from Family Magazine of 1740, directs that the sauce for a roast stuffed chine of pork be "made with lemon-peel, apples, sugar, butter, and mustard." This would have been one of those sweet-sharp sauces, something like Italian fruit mustards, which for centuries have been associated with rich, fat meat such as pork. A chine was a cut from the back of a pig, rather like a joint of back bacon in the piece. There is a high proportion of fat on a chine, so the apple and mustard sauce was an appropriate one.

✤ BREAD SAUCE ✦

I do not willingly cook or eat bread sauce, but recognize that there are still many people to whom the turkey without bread sauce is not the turkey. (An Italian friend of mine once told me that in Sardinia a peasant woman had said to her, "Christmas without a roast cat wouldn't be Christmas." Each to his tradition.) So here is a way of making it acceptable. A warning, though. My recipe calls for home-made bread or, failing that, bread bought from an independent baker, who knows what bread is and also produces it. Factory bread simply won't do. I don't often make white bread, but every now and then it is needed to make croûtons for soup, crumbs for stuffings and so on, so when Christmas looms I make a couple of white loaves and keep them in the freezer against the day.

To make about I pint of sauce the ingredients are a slice of home-made white bread weighing approximately 2oz (less rather than more) without crust, I pint of creamy milk, 10 white peppercorns, 10 coriander seeds, 1 shallot or very small onion, 3 tablespoons of cream.

Cut the crusts from the slice of bread before you weigh it. Reduce the bread to crumbs in the blender or food processor. Turn the crumbs into a bowl.

Put the milk, spices, and peeled shallot or onion into a

heavy stainless steel or non-stick saucepan and bring to a simmer over very low heat. Watch it. After 5 minutes strain the milk over the bread crumbs, and either discard the shallot and spices or keep them for some other purpose such as stock. Leave for about 15 minutes so that the bread has a chance to swell. Return the mixture to your rinsed-out saucepan. Set this over a trivet or a griddle, so that it is raised above the direct heat, whether gas or electricity. Let the sauce cook very, very slowly. Stand over it, stirring fairly frequently. For a while it looks hopelessly thin. Don't panic and add more bread. In a little time, as the bread swells more and more, the sauce thickens. In about 15 minutes it will reach the right consistency, thick and creamy. It may even be necessary to add a little extra milk. I aim to achieve a thickish pouring sauce, but not a poultice. You will probably need to add salt and a little freshly milled white pepper, or if you have it celery salt. Finally, stir in the cream. Pour the hot sauce into the top part of a double saucepan and keep it warm over simmering water until the moment comes to transfer it to a warmed sauceboat or bowl and hand it round with the turkey.

Notes

1. Don't ever attempt to cook bread sauce in an enameled pan. It will stick, and the pan will be troublesome to clean.

2. The sauce can be made a day or two in advance, stored in a covered bowl in the refrigerator and reheated in a double saucepan.

3. A little chopped raw celery stirred into the sauce while it is reheating is, to my mind, a great improvement.

4. Some old recipes specify a meat or giblet stock rather than milk as the basis for bread sauce. If you use this you won't need the shallot and spices. Just pour the hot stock over the bread crumbs and go on from there.

⇥ CRANBERRY SAUCE ⇤

Cook the berries with a little water in a covered saucepan. When cooked, pound them and pass them through a hair sieve. To the purée thus obtained add soft sugar to taste, a little pepper and enough of the water in which the cranberries have cooked to obtain the consistency of a thick sauce.

MARCEL BOULESTIN
The Evening Standard Book of Menus, 1935

⇥ CUMBERLAND SAUCE ⇤

What basis there is for the story that Cumberland sauce was named after Ernest, Duke of Cumberland, that brother of George IV's who became the last independent ruler of Hanover, nobody has ever explained. Still, as legends concerning the origin of dishes go, it's as good as another and better than some: the sauce itself being as obviously German in origin as was its supposed royal namesake of the House of Hanover. All the same, it is odd that no recipe for Cumberland sauce as such appears in any of the mid- or late-nineteenth-century standard cookery books in which one might expect to find it.

Eliza Acton's Modern Cookery, *1845, doesn't mention it; neither does Mrs. Beeton's* Household Management, *1861; nor Francatelli's* Cook's Guide *of the Eighties. When the recipe does get into print it is in a book about English cooking written in French by a Frenchman, a chef called Alfred Suzanne, who had*

worked in two great English households of the period, those of the Duke of Bedford and of the Earl of Wilton. Possibly in one of these aristocratic kitchens the sauce, probably already familiar, had been renamed in honor of a royal visit or some such festivity. In any case, it is the recipe in Suzanne's book La Cuisine Anglaise, *1904, which seems to have been popularized in the Edwardian period by Escoffier, who was also responsible for its commercial success. Another respected French writer, Ali-Bab, describes a similar mixture of redcurrant jelly, port and orange peel which, he says, is called Sauce Victoria, asserting that it is served with grouse.*

Was it that it took French cooks to perceive the possibilities of a sauce so very alien to French cooking? Evidently. At any rate, another great chef and writer of French birth, Alexis Soyer, had in fact preceded his compatriots by fifty years. What is without doubt Cumberland sauce, although a rather simpler version than the one most of us know nowadays, is incorporated in a three-page recipe for boar's head given in this author's Gastronomic Regenerator, *1853.*

Acknowledged by Soyer to be the German method of making a sauce to be eaten with boar's head (Suzanne, Escoffier and Prosper Montagne all give it as the characteristic English accompaniment to a haunch of venison; it is also perfect with cold tongue and ham), his instructions are to "cut the rind, free from pith, of two Seville oranges into very thin strips half an inch in length, which blanch in boiling water, drain them upon a sieve and put them into a basin, with a spoonful of mixed English mustard, four of currant jelly, a little pepper, salt (mix well together) and half a pint of good port wine."

Among Soyer's extraordinarily versatile gifts was his great capacity for devising simple recipes of this kind, recipes that are quite timeless and that anyone with no more than a single gas ring to cook on could still use today. (His Shilling Cookery for the People, *1855, is a little mine of instructive information for a lone, unskilled and impecunious cook.) And as far as Cumberland sauce is concerned, Soyer's recipe is the one I habitually use these days; it produces results which, if anything, are better than Suzanne's more complicated formula – he and Escoffier both add shallots, which are unnecessary. The only alterations I make are to use French mustard instead of English and to reduce the quantity of port; ½ pint to 4 tablespoons of jelly produces a sauce which would be excessively liquid for modern tastes, although it probably suited Soyer's contemporaries.*

This best of all sauces for cold meat – ham, pressed beef, tongue, venison, boar's head or pork brawn – can be made in small quantities and in a quick and economical way as follows.

With a potato parer cut the rind, very thinly, from 2 large oranges. Slice this into matchstick strips. Plunge them into boiling water and let them boil 5 minutes. Strain them.

Put them in a bowl with 4 tablespoons of redcurrant jelly, a heaped teaspoon of yellow Dijon mustard, a little freshly milled pepper, a pinch of salt and optionally a sprinkling of ground ginger.

Place this bowl over a saucepan of water, and heat, stirring all the time, until the jelly is melted and the mustard smooth. It may be necessary at this stage to sieve the jelly in order to smooth out the globules that will not dissolve. Return the sieved jelly to the bowl standing over its pan of hot water.

Now add 7-8 tablespoons of medium tawny port. Stir and cook for another 5 minutes. Serve cold. There will be enough for 4 people.

Made in double or triple quantities this sauce can be stored in covered jars and will keep for several weeks.

Note

On no account should corn flour, gelatin or any other stiffening be added to Cumberland sauce. The mixture thickens as it cools, and the sauce is invariably served cold, even with a hot ham or tongue.

✧ Cumberland Sauce (Cooked Version) ✦

4 oranges, 2 lemons, 1lb of redcurrant jelly, ¼ pint of port, 2½ fl oz of mild wine vinegar, 1 dessertspoon of French mustard, about 2 tablespoons of white sugar, a pinch of ground ginger, salt and pepper.

Peel the oranges and lemons very thinly, without a trace of pith. The easiest way to do this is with an ordinary potato parer.

With a small sharp knife cut the peel in thin strips no wider than matches and about the same length. Plunge into boiling water, boil 5 minutes, and strain. The object of this operation is to remove the bitter taste from the peel.

Now melt the jelly in a thick pan, and when it is warm add the port, the vinegar which has been thoroughly blended with the mustard (otherwise the mustard has a tendency to separate into lumps) and the sugar, ginger, and a pinch of salt and black pepper. Stir in the strained juice of the oranges and lemons. If by this time the jelly has not fully dissolved the mixture must be sieved and then returned to the rinsed-out pan. Bring to the boil, skim. When all the scum has been removed add the blanched peel, and cook for about 20 minutes, until the whole mixture thickens to a syrup-like consistency. Test it on a plate, as for jam. It should be firm enough not to run, but not set as a jelly.

If you use home-made redcurrant jelly, the sauce will take a little longer to thicken, as commercial jelly is usually more solid to start with. The exact amount of sugar to be used depends upon the relative sweetness of the jelly, and also on the type of port used.

To store the sauce, simply pour it into wide-mouthed bottles or jars and seal as for jam. It thickens slightly as it matures. This amount fills two 1lb jars.

To make seven jars the quantities are 16 oranges, 6 large lemons, 4lb of redcurrant jelly, I pint of port, 8fl oz of wine vinegar, 2 tablespoons of French mustard, 8oz of sugar, ½ teaspoon of ground ginger, and salt and pepper.

The method is the same as for the smaller quantity, but for this amount the cooking time is about 40 minutes.

✦ ORANGE SAUCE FOR TONGUE, HAM, OR WILD DUCK ✦
*This formula contains much the same ingredients as Cumberland
sauce, but is made in a different way. It is as good hot with hot
tongue or ham or wild duck as with cold meats. It is a sauce I have
evolved from recipes given by Georgiana Countess of Dudley in*
The Dudley Recipe Book, *1909, and by Dorothy Allhusen
in her* Book of Scents and Dishes, *1927.*

2 oranges, 1 lemon, ½lb of redcurrant jelly, 2-3 teaspoons of Dijon mustard, H teaspoon of salt, 4 tablespoons of port.

Grate the rinds of the oranges and the lemon on a coarse grater. Squeeze and strain the juice of one of the oranges and of half the lemon. Melt the jelly in the top half of a double saucepan or in a bowl standing in a pan of simmering water. Stir in the other ingredients, the fruit rinds and the mustard and salt first, then the fruit juices and lastly the port. Continue stirring over steam until all ingredients are well blended. Rub through a fine sieve. Stored in covered jam jars or sauce bottles this orange sauce will keep a long while. If to be served hot, the sauce should be reheated over steam, not over direct heat.

→ OXFORD SAUCE ←
This sauce is excellent with cold spiced or salt beef (see "Meats")
and with a beef loaf (see "Cold Meats").

Put 2 tablespoons of soft dark brown sugar in a bowl or mortar. Stir in 2 teaspoons of made mustard. Add a half teaspoon each of salt and freshly milled pepper. Stir in, gradually, as for mayonnaise, 5-6 tablespoons of olive oil. Finally, add 2 tablespoons of wine vinegar.

In appearance and consistency the sauce should be reminiscent of thick dark honey; in taste it is sweet-sharp, in other words *egurdouce*.

→ ALSATIAN SAUCE FOR HARE OR VENISON ←

Put in a small saucepan a glass of port wine with a pinch of nutmeg, salt and pepper. Reduce by one third; add twice the quantity of redcurrant jelly, previously melted, a tablespoonful of grated horseradish, a little cream, stir well, cook for one minute more and serve.

This is a recipe given by Marcel Boulestin in *The Evening Standard Book of Menus*, published in 1935. I use ¼lb of jelly and interpret "a glass of port" as about ⅛ of a pint. If the sauce is for cold ham, gammon or tongue, I sieve it, and omit the cream.

→ SWEET-SOUR CHERRY SAUCE FOR COLD TONGUE ←

Ingredients are ½lb of bottled, tinned or fresh cherries, ½lb of redcurrant or rowanberry jelly, 2 teaspoons of French mustard, 3 tablespoons of wine vinegar, freshly milled pepper.

Stone the cherries, and if they are large halve them. In a bowl over boiling water melt the jelly. Stir in the mustard, then the vinegar, and a little pepper. When the jelly is liquid and smooth add the cherries. Serve cold.

Notes

1. When using commercial red currant jelly for sauces it is often necessary, or at any rate desirable, to sieve it after it has melted and before adding the solid ingredients. Otherwise a few undissolved globules of jelly may remain in the finished sauce. In any case it is always preferable to melt the jelly by the bain-marie system rather than over direct heat, for if allowed to come to the boil the jelly will produce a scum of which it is difficult to rid the finished sauce.

2. In the summer when fresh cherries are in season use, if you can find them, the dark juicy variety which the French call bigarreaux.

✧ MAYONNAISE ✧

Mayonnaise is one of the best and most useful sauces in existence, but because it is not cooked at all the making of it seems to represent to the uninitiated something in the nature of magic, or at least of a successful conjuring trick, although the mystery has been somewhat diminished by the advent of electric mixers and the fact that a beautiful thick mayonnaise can be produced from the liquidizer in a matter of a minute or two. But although I regard this machine with the utmost gratitude, since it is a mechanical kitchen-maid rather than a gadget, I do not care, unless I am in a great hurry, to let it deprive me of the pleasure and satisfaction to be obtained from sitting down quietly with bowl and spoon, eggs and oil, to the peaceful kitchen task of concocting the beautiful shining golden ointment which is mayonnaise.

1. Proportions, to make it really easy, and for 6 plentiful helpings, are 3 egg yolks (although you can easily make do with

2 when you have a little experience) to about ½ pint of olive oil. Half a teaspoon of salt, a few drops of tarragon or wine vinegar or the juice of half a lemon at most.

2. If the oil has become congealed in cold weather, stand the bottle in a warm room to thaw very gradually and do not use it until it is once more quite limpid and clear. Frozen oil will curdle the sauce as sure as fate. But also it must not be too warm. In tropical climates the oil has to be cooled on ice before a mayonnaise is made.

3. Stand the bowl in which the mayonnaise is to be made on a damp cloth or newspaper to prevent its sliding about. Use a wooden spoon for stirring.

4. Whisk or stir the yolks pretty thoroughly before starting to add the oil, which is best poured out into a measuring jug, so that you can see just how much you are using.

5. Add salt, then the oil, drop by drop at first, but with 3 yolks the drops can quickly be turned into a slow, thin stream. It is only, with this quantity of eggs, when about a third of the oil has gone in that the mayonnaise starts coming to life and acquiring its characteristic solidity. After this it should, if a spoonful is lifted up and dropped back into the bowl, fall from the spoon with a satisfying plop, and retain its shape, like a thick jelly.

6. Add the vinegar from time to time from a dropper or a tea-spoon, not straight from the bottle, or you risk ruining the whole thing by adding more than you intended.

7. If it is more convenient to make the mayonnaise a day, or even two or three days, beforehand, stir in at the very last 2 tablespoons of boiling water. The mayonnaise will then nei-ther separate nor turn oily on the surface. Keep it in a cool place, but not in the refrigerator.

PICKLES AND CHUTNEYS

→ SWEET-SOUR TOMATO AND ORANGE PICKLE ←
This is a pickle that can be made at any time and with almost any tomatoes, although very firm and slightly unripe ones are the best. Half and half green and red tomatoes produce good results.

1½lb of sugar, ½ pint of tarragon vinegar, 2lb of firm tomatoes, 2 small oranges.

In a preserving pan (preferably an aluminum one – don't use an untinned copper jam pan for pickles or chutneys) boil the sugar and vinegar to a thin syrup.

Pour boiling water over the tomatoes. Skin and chop them. Slice the oranges, peel included, first into thin rounds, then cut each round in 4 pieces, discarding all pips and the ends of the oranges.

Put the chopped tomatoes and oranges into the hot syrup, bring to the boil. Continue the boiling, at a moderate pace, skimming from time to time, for about 45 minutes to 1 hour, according to quantity, until the mixture sets when a little is dropped on to a plate.

Pack into small jars. This is good with cold pork, gammon and ham and also with cold salt beef or the Pork and Veal Loaf in the "Cold Meats" chapter.

Note
When the pickle is to be made in quantity the easiest way of preparing the tomatoes is to pack them in a big earthenware pot and let them

soften in a low oven for half an hour or a little longer. Then push the whole batch through a coarse sieve or mouli-légumes.

↦ SWEET-SOUR PEARS ↤

An excellent mild pickle that will keep a few days but is intended for current consumption rather than for storing. The method used is the same as that in the recipe for Pears Baked in Wine (see "Desserts"), but the result is utterly different.

You need 3–4lb of small cooking pears, 6–8oz of sugar, ½ pint of cider vinegar, a strip of orange peel.

Peel the pears but leave the stalks on. Put them in a glazed earthenware oven pot, add the sugar and vinegar and the orange peel. Pour in just enough water to cover the pears. Put a lid on the pot and cook in a moderate oven, 325°F, until they are deep golden yellow and so soft that they can be easily pierced with a skewer. This may take anything from 2½ to 5 hours according to the variety of pears you are using.

Pour off the juice into a big wide pan and boil it rapidly until all you have left is a small amount of thick syrup.

Arrange the pears in a pyramid in a bowl. Pour over the syrup. Serve with cold pressed beef, ham, pork or gammon.

↦ SPICED QUINCES ↤

Peel and core the quinces, cut each into about 8 pieces. Cover them with cold water and add a small handful of coarse salt. Boil quickly for 10 minutes and strain. To each 1 pint of this juice add 1lb of white sugar, ¼ pint of Orléans or wine vinegar, and a teaspoon of whole coriander seeds; bring to the boil, put in the fruit and simmer until the slices are tender. Next day drain off the syrup, bring it to the boil, pour it back over the quinces packed into preserving jars, and screw or clip down the covers while still warm.

These spiced quinces are excellent to eat with boiled bacon, cold or hot, with pork, with mutton, and with cold turkey.

It is worth noting, especially now that quinces have become rather rare and unfamiliar to English cooks, that the fruit is at its best when picked slightly unripe and left to mature in a warm kitchen. When the fruit is yellow and the scent – it is unmistakable – is fully developed, cook the quinces without further delay. If left too long the flesh becomes cottony, does not absorb the sugar, and gives a dry leathery preserve. Spiced quinces keep a long time.

✣ PUMPKIN AND TOMATO CHUTNEY ✣

It is not generally known that pumpkin can make an excellent chutney, rich and dark. The recipe below produces a mixture with a taste which is spicy but not too sharp; the pumpkin slices retain something of their shape, and shine translucently through the glass jars.

Greengrocers very often sell pumpkins by the piece; a whole one is, of course, cheaper, but remember that once it is cut it will not keep longer than about ten days.

Ingredients are a 2½lb piece of pumpkin (gross weight), 1lb of ripe tomatoes, ½lb of onions, 2 cloves of garlic, 2oz of sultanas, ¾lb each of soft dark brown sugar and white caster sugar, 2 tablespoons of salt, 2 scant teaspoons each of ground ginger, black peppercorns and allspice berries, 1¼ pints of wine vinegar or cider vinegar.

Peel the pumpkin, discard seeds and cottony center. Slice, then cut into pieces roughly 2 inches wide and long and ½ inch thick. Pour boiling water over the tomatoes, skin and slice them. Peel and slice the onions and the garlic.

Put all solid ingredients, including spices (crush the peppercorns and allspice berries in a mortar) and sugar, in your preserving pan. (For chutneys, always use heavy aluminum, never untinned copper jam pans.) Add vinegar. Bring gently to the boil, and then cook steadily, but not at a gallop, until the mixture is jammy. Skim from time to time, and toward the end of the cooking, which will take altogether about 50 minutes, stir very frequently. Chutney can be a disastrous sticker if you don't give it your full attention during the final stages.

This is a long-keeping chutney, but, like most chutneys, it is best if cooked to a moderate set only; in other words it should still be a little bit runny; if too solid it will quickly dry up.

Ladle into pots, which should be filled right to the brim. When cold cover with rounds of waxed paper, and then with a double layer of thick greaseproof paper. (Or use jars with plastic-lined lids that will not be corroded by vinegar. JN.) Transparent covers that let in the light are not suitable for chutney.

The yield from these quantities will be approximately 3½lb; and although it may be a little more extravagant as regards fuel and materials, I find chutney cooked in small batches more satisfactory than when produced on a large scale.

It is worth noting that should it be more convenient, all ingredients for the chutney can be prepared, mixed with the sugar and vinegar, and left for several hours or overnight (but not longer than 12 hours) in a covered bowl before cooking.

✳ Lemons for Christmas ✳

We had two most welcome gifts. Food, of course. One was a cockerel, the other a tin box containing twenty-nine lemons, sent by a soldier in the Middle East. How we called down blessings on his head as we dis-

cussed the rival merits of lemon pie, lemon cheese, lemon marmalade, gin and lemon, lemon juice in our salad dressing, and grated lemon-peel in the stuffing of the cockerel. Even with twenty-nine lemons we had to limit our aspirations, so we finally decided on a lemon pie, lemon marmalade, and lemon-peel in the stuffing. Then we would see. How lucky it was that the lemons came when we had our extra rations of margarine and sugar. We had to make some lemon marmalade because we are perennially short of marmalade. One pound does not spin out for breakfast for three people for a month, spread we never so thin, and our grocer refuses to allow us more. "Two jams: one mar." is his stern ruling from which he never departs.

I do not know if we shall manage a lemon pie, for, on looking it up in the Concise Encyclopedia of Gastronomy, I was shocked to find it omitted from this invaluable work. Wot! No lemon pie? With its deep layer of celandine-yellow curd and sea-foam meringue top tinted a delicate biscuit-color on the fragile peaks (see how lyrical I become at the very thought), it is worthy of a place in any list of sweetmeats, even a concise one. Sadly I reflect that in all probability I cannot run a recipe to earth now, for – unmitigated fool that I was – I threw all the more elaborate cookery books that we possessed to salvage in 1940, because I had not realized then what I know to my cost now, that all the most valuable hints for making wartime food palatable, even with all the current limitations, are to be found in such books, and not in the useless and frequently revolting recipes published by the Ministry of Food. Strange, but true.

JOYCE CONYNGHAM GREEN
Salmagundi, J. M. Dent, 1947

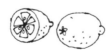

Desserts

———— ⋘ · X · ⋙ ————

Plum Pottage, Porridge, Broth and Pudding

LTHOUGH PLUM PUDDINGS were in the cookery books by the first half of the seventeenth century and obviously quite common by the middle of the eighteenth, they seem not to have been specifically associated with Christmas until the early decades of the nineteenth. Plum porridges and pottages – the terms seem to have been interchangeable – on the other hand, certainly were Christmas specialties during the eighteenth century and were served at the beginning of the meal. Plum porridge, at any rate according to Hannah Glasse's recipe in *The Art of Cooking Made Plain and Easy*, 4th Edition, 1751, was a gruel made with barley grains, raisins and currants boiled in water until thick, then spiced, sweetened with sugar and enriched with white wine. Another very similar version was made on a basis of oatmeal. Both were clearly variations and elaborations on the very ancient fermity or frumenty, the dish of boiled wheat grain enriched with milk, cream and eggs common to most of the wheat-growing countries of Europe, and regarded as a very special dish for festivals and banquets. To the rich, frumenty became the almost obligatory accompaniment to roast venison; to yeomen, farmers and humbler country people, wheat was a luxury, and frumenty a treat at Christmas and other special celebrations. It is indeed a very delicious and richly flavored mixture, and although it wasn't then served as a dessert, I would now find it a good deal preferable to our present Christmas pudding.

Wheat was, of course, the most highly prized of all the cereal grains and I fancy that Hannah Glasse's plum porridges and gruels owe something to her origins in Northumberland, where oats and barley were the staple grains until late in the eighteenth century.

Plum porridge for Christmas, however, was something very different again from plum porridge based on whole barley grains or coarse oatmeal. Hannah Glasse's recipe for this special porridge calls for a broth made from a leg and shin of beef boiled in 8 gallons of water. The strained broth was to be thickened with slices of bread from 6 penny loaves – a penny loaf should probably be reckoned as weighing about ½lb if made from finely bolted flour, three times that if made from coarse meal – first steeped and then boiled in a portion of the broth. This was strained and returned to the main batch of broth, which was then reheated prior to the addition of 5lb each of currants and raisins and 2lb of "pruens" cooked separately until tender. The fruit is followed into the pot by 1oz of mace, ½oz of cloves, 2 nutmegs, all beat fine, 3lb of sugar, a little salt, a quart each of sack and claret and the juice of 3 lemons. The whole fearsome brew was poured "into earthen Pans and keep them for Use." Interestingly, this recipe, which appears in Mrs. Glasse's soup and broth chapter, is suspiciously similar to the one given by E. Smith, *The Complete Housewife*, 1753 Edition, first published 1727, the significant difference being that the Smith recipe was called simply Plumb Porridge while the Glasse version is specifically entitled Plumb Porridge for Christmas. Both were certainly regarded as pottages rather than puddings. Indeed, even with 12lb of fruit and a substantial thickening of bread, the mixture would still have been fairly liquid, and although often claimed as the ancestor of our Christmas pudding, it figured at the beginning of the meal, as evidenced, for example, by the dinner given to thirteen guests by Timothy Burrell, squire of Ockendon House, Cuckfield, Sussex on New Year's Day, 1707, and recorded in his diary.

This meal consisted of three dishes of "Plumm Pottage," a calf's head and bacon, a goose, a pig – presumably a suckling pig – a sirloin of roast beef, a loin of veal, a second goose, a boiled clod of beef, two baked puddings (plum puddings? alas, we are not told), three dishes of minced pies, two capons, two dishes of tarts, two pullets. It's difficult to be sure in what order the dishes were served, but they were probably put upon the table in three separate services, each one constituting a hefty meal in itself. The general rule at the time was boiled meats first (after the pottage), baked next, roasted last. From the way squire Burrell noted it all down, it looks very much as if this were the pattern followed, with three dishes of plumm pottage arranged at intervals round the table, followed by the calf's head and any boiled meats and poultry, the guests helping themselves. When this lot was devoured, the dishes would have been removed by servants and replaced by the roast meats, including probably two roast geese. The pullets, the puddings, the mince pies and the tarts – quite a light snack – would all have been the third course. If the host himself were doing all the carving, as was usually the custom at the time, he must have had little chance to eat anything himself. And, of course, all the food would have been tepid by the time it reached the plates of the guests. That was also perfectly usual, and meals on this pattern continued as part of English country life until late in Victoria's reign. Two dinners for his tenant farmers, not Christmas or New Year meals in name, but made up of much the same festive dishes, and given in 1878 and 1879 by the Reverend Francis Kilvert, the now famous diarist and vicar of Clyro near Hay-on-Wye, provide a very good idea of the way these things were arranged. The fare was nothing like as gross as squire Burrell's, but was certainly still plentiful enough. The plum pottage, however, had long gone, the Victorian tradition of turkey as well as roast beef (not to mention beefsteak pie as well) followed by plum pudding, mince pies and other sweet things being well established.

A little less forbidding than Hannah Glasse's is the following recipe:

To make Plumm-Pottage

Take two gallons of strong broth, put into it two pounds of currans, two pounds of raisins of the sun, half an ounce of sweet spice, one pound of sugar, a quart of claret, a pint of canary; squeeze three seville-oranges and three lemons into it, and thicken it with rice, flour, and a pound of prunes.

The Family Magazine, 1740, page 46

DESERTS

✣ THE PUDDING ✤

I recounted in *Spices, Salt and Aromatics in the English Kitchen* how, when I was living on the island of Syros in the Cyclades, my village neighbors nagged me into making a Christmas pudding for them. The ingredients were, of course, all to hand. There were luscious local raisins, sun-dried, currants from Zante, almonds from the mainland, citron grown and candied on a neighboring island, beef suet from the town butcher (town was the port of Syra five miles away by donkey ride), Greek-made brandy. The eggs were new-laid. It all sounds simple enough. Well, first the suet had to be skinned and shredded, all by hand. The raisins had to be stoned, also by hand. They were very gooey and stuck to my fingers. The citron peel was infinitely superior to anything we can buy here. To cut it up into tiny pieces was another matter. I didn't have a good knife in my primitive kitchen, and with a blunt one the job was incredibly difficult. There was bread to be grated for crumbs. Nowadays, we can simply throw a few slices of bread into an electric chopper or food processor, and it's all done in a minute. Thirty years ago it took ages, and was one of the most boring of all kitchen tasks.

At last, after two long days in the kitchen, the ingredients were just about ready. To give the pudding a preliminary boiling of 3 or 4 hours it was necessary to keep constant watch on my charcoal fire, fanning and refueling at frequent intervals for fear the fire should get too low and the water go off the boil. At the end of 2 hours I transferred the pudding in its basin (I had borrowed this uniquely English necessity from the British Consul's household) to a hay box constructed, with the help of the villagers, expressly for the purpose. There it stayed from early afternoon to suppertime, when my Christmas party got under way. By the time we reached the moment to extract the pudding from its box it was scarcely more than tepid. Under the circumstances that didn't matter in the least. The Greeks dislike and distrust hot food, and the islanders were merely curious to know what the English Christmas pudding was like. I must admit that with all the beautiful ingredients I'd used, it was quite creditable, although I think my village friends were somewhat mystified, as much by the hay box as by the unfamiliar nature of the pudding itself.

What I had learned from going through the lengthy business of preparing all the ingredients by hand was some understanding of the tedious jobs the cooks and kitchen-maids of the past were obliged to perform. So when I hear people moaning about packet suet and raisins and currants and peel and how much better all these things were in the old days, when everything was hand-prepared, I wonder if they themselves have ever given a thought to what it was like to shred suet, clean currants, take the stones out of huge sticky raisins, chop tough, gummy candied citron and orange peel, pound all the spices in a mortar and sieve them. Myself, although I agree that today's ingredients are not a patch on those I found in Greece, which was after all the original source of most of our dried fruits, I find Christmas plum pudding a pretty awful concoction, and have not made one since that epic occasion on Syros (that was some thirty-five years ago), and hope very much I shall never again have to.

The recipe I used in those far-off days was my elder sister's – I had telegraphed home for it – one of those in which there was 2lb of practically everything. I have lost the original, a few scribbled notes on the back of an envelope, recording the principal ingredients in *okes* – the Greek 3lb unit – being all that remain. So here, instead, is a similar one from Eleanor

Jenkinson's *The Ocklye Cookery Book*, a pre-1914 family recipe book of particular charm.

Miss Jenkinson was the daughter of a clergyman, the Reverend John Jenkinson, for whom she kept house at Ocklye, Crowborough, Sussex, until he died in 1914, at the age of ninety-one. Her niece, Mrs. Jean Pace, wrote to me in 1971: "I remember Aunt Nelly well; she was a splendid old lady, lean, weather-beaten, betweeded, a keen gardener and naturalist and a great music-lover. . . . I treasure my battered copy of her cookery book, which recalls meals enjoyed in childhood, particularly those luscious puddings, while Athol Brose was traditionally served at family music-parties." Miss Jenkinson's brother Francis, Cambridge University Librarian from 1889 to 1923, was incidentally responsible for introducing the recipe for *crème brûlée* to the kitchens of Trinity College Cambridge, where it became famous. The story is told by Miss Jenkinson herself, although without naming her brother.

Friends who have used the Ocklye Christmas pudding recipe since I reproduced it in *Spices, Salt and Aromatics* in 1970 have been well pleased with it. Note that no sugar is required. The pudding is all the better for the omission, the dried fruit providing more than enough of its own natural sweetness. But I have a distinct recollection of stout or old ale as well as brandy and rum being called for in my recipe, and on an Aegean island that was a bit of a puzzle. I suspect that in the end I settled for brandy instead. In the Ocklye recipe ½ pint of stout could be substituted for an equal quantity of the milk, and would enhance both flavor and color.

The 14 hours boiling, by the way, is for unusually large puddings. With nearly 10lb of ingredients all told, Miss Jenkinson's cook was evidently allowing for two puddings of 5lb each, so all those hours of boiling wouldn't have been excessive. For smaller puddings see "Notes on the Boiling or Steaming," and also the Buckland recipe that follows the Ocklye one.

Two pounds and a quarter of stoned raisins, two pounds and a quarter of currants, six ounces of finely-chopped candied peel, thirteen eggs, one pint and a half of milk, one teacupful and a half of bread crumbs, one pound and a half of flour, one pound and a half of finely-chopped suet, three wineglasses of brandy, two wineglasses of rum.

Mix these ingredients well together, put into buttered basins, and boil for fourteen hours. The quantity makes two large puddings.

ELEANOR L. JENKINSON
The Ocklye Cookery Book, 1909

✧ THE BUCKLAND PLUM PUDDING ✧
Here is another family recipe, described by the author as "our own plum pudding." This one calls for sugar, although I think it could quite well be omitted.

1lb of best beef suet chopped very fine, 1lb best raisins stoned and cut in half, 1lb of currants well washed and dried, ½lb of flour, ½lb of finely crumbled bread crumbs, ½lb mixed candied peel finely shred, ½lb of white sugar pounded and sifted, a little lemon peel grated, a small teaspoonful of mixed spice and half a nutmeg, the juice of half a lemon, 3 eggs well beaten, and ¼ pint of brandy.

Mix all the dry ingredients together thoroughly with a wooden spoon, then add the eggs, brandy, and lemon, with enough cold water to make a rather stiff compound. Put into well-buttered basins, cover with buttered paper and a well-floured cloth, and boil for eight or nine hours.

We generally make treble quantity for Christmas, boiling all the puddings at the same time – nine hours, hang the basins in the kitchen (not to touch the wall) and they will keep for months. When wanted for use, boil an hour, taking care not to allow the water to rise to the top of the basin, or covering the basin with another well-wetted and floured cloth.

ANNE BUCKLAND
Our Viands, London, 1893

Notes on the Mixing and Packing

1. For mixing the pudding you need a really capacious bowl and a stout wooden spoon – and as everybody in the family is supposed to take a hand in the job, this part of it shouldn't be very hard work. It's all done the day before the puddings are to be cooked, and the mixture left overnight in the covered bowl, in a cool place. Some people consider it a mistake to add the brandy, rum and ale until the next day, but it's easier to do all the mixing in one go. In a single night the fruit isn't going to start fermenting.

2. The ritual silver coins, ring, thimble, and other pudding favors can be put into each pudding when the basins are packed – they're supposed to be wrapped in greaseproof paper, more so that they can be easily found than for hygienic reasons. But if there are small children it's better to slip them surreptitiously on the plates when the pudding is served so that they are easily seen. The drama of inadvertently swallowed coins and charms is something one can do without on Christmas Day.

3. The pudding will swell during the cooking, so allow for this by leaving an inch or so of space at the top when the mixture is packed into the buttered basins.

4. Cover each pudding with buttered greaseproof paper before tying on the cloths.

Notes on the Boiling or Steaming

1. Originally, plum puddings, as indeed all puddings, were boiled in floured cloths in cauldrons suspended over the fire. If large, they were boiled in the copper used for boiling the wash. This was a built-in copper vessel of several gallons' capacity heated by a fire underneath. When the water boiled, the puddings suspended from a stout stick or pole were lowered into it, and the stick left across the copper so that when done they could be easily lifted out again. By this means the puddings round as a great ball were achieved. Whether they were always so perfectly round and faultless as depicted in the old illustrations I can't help doubting. Turning them out of the cloths was clearly a tricky and messy operation, and many a pudding must have collapsed in the process. Lady Hanover, for one, observed that when the puddings were boiled in cloths, the water became a sort of raisin and currant soup and that the waste of ingredients was considerable.

With the coming of mass-produced cheap pudding basins, and the steaming rather than boiling of puddings, the whole business became much easier, and even if the puddings didn't look quite so picturesque, turning them out of the basins was comparatively painless. Eliza Acton, however, held that "plum puddings, which it is customary to boil in moulds, are both lighter and less dry, when closely tied in stout cloths well buttered and floured." If to be boiled in a big saucepan, Miss Acton recommended that a plate be put at the bottom of the pan, so that the pudding could rest on it and need not be kept floating.

2. Nowadays, most people find the most practical method of steaming puddings is to stand the basins on a rack or trivet – an iron griddle for example – in the pan, or if several puddings are to be cooked at once to use a fish kettle which has its own rack.

3. Start the puddings off in boiling water, enough to come about two-thirds of the way up the sides of the basins. Cover the pan and leave it for about 2 hours before taking a look. Have a kettle of water ready boiling in case the water needs topping up, and keep the water on the boil, as much as possible at the same level, for the entire cooking time

– that is 4 hours for 1 pint basins, 6 hours for 1H pint basins and 7-8 hours for 2 pint basins. These are the minimum times; longer cooking will do no harm.

4. When you lift the puddings from the water leave them to cool a little, then unknot the cloths, rinse and dry them thoroughly, but don't remove the underneath covering of greaseproof paper. (Foil isn't advisable as a long-term pudding covering. The acid content of the puddings is likely to attack the foil, and mould can follow.) Leave the puddings overnight, so that they are completely cooled. Replace the dry cloths and store the puddings in a dry and cool place.

5. On the day give the pudding a good 2 hours of steaming. When you take it out of the water let it stand about 10 minutes before attempting to turn it out.

The Ritual Flames and the Sauce

Before attempting to set light to the brandy or rum – I should advise rum, or even whisky if you have it; both are cheaper than brandy – the spirit must be warmed in a small saucepan. Put a match to it and pour it flaming over the pudding on its hot dish. Don't forget a pretty sprig of holly for the top. The recipe for brandy butter follows.

⇾ BRANDY BUTTER ⇽

For about a dozen helpings the ingredients are: 1lb of unsalted butter, 8oz of icing sugar, 2 or 3 tablespoons of brandy, a sprinkling of nutmeg, a teaspoon of lemon juice.

If you have an electric blender, simply cut up the butter and put it with all the other ingredients into the goblet and let them whizz away for 2 or 3 minutes. You get a better amalgamated and smoother sauce than you can ever get by hand.

For those who haven't a mixer the most successful procedure seems to me to be as follows: soften your butter by putting it into a warmed bowl. In another bowl, also warmed, mix the icing, sugar, brandy, nutmeg and lemon juice to a smooth cream.

Beat the butter, if possible in a big wooden mixing bowl and with a wooden fork, to a soft cream; very gradually add the sugar and brandy mixture and stir or knead by hand until the butter is smooth. Store in a covered dish, or turn into jars, press down, and store in the refrigerator.

It is quite hard work mixing brandy butter by hand in any quantity, but it can be done in ½lb batches. And if you don't eat Christmas pudding, have it with an outsize mince pie made in a flan or tart tin. And it is lovely with hot apple pie, instead of cream.

Readers familiar with brandy butter recipes will see that the proportions usually recommended – twice the weight of sugar to butter – are reversed in this recipe. This is because many people, myself included, find the normal brandy butter much too sweet. But whatever proportions are used, the method of making the sauce is the same.

→ PROFESSOR HARDY'S SAUCE ←
In Edwardian cookery books brandy butter is often called Senior Wrangler sauce, and in an excellent 1930s collection of recipes

published by the Daily Telegraph *I came across the following
note and recipe. Was Professor Hardy the inventive
Senior Wrangler concerned?*

This recipe was "composed" by Mr. Hardy, member of Sidney Sussex
College, Cambridge, and was usually called Professor Hardy's sauce.
It is the foundation of the brandy butter now served.

Take ¼lb of butter and rather more of finely powdered sugar, beat
them well together till quite white and light. Then add a little grated
nutmeg, 1 tablespoon of brandy, and 2 of sherry (these must be added
slowly, by degrees, beating thoroughly all the time until mixed). Serve
very cold piled up in a glass cup or boat.

"Four Hundred Prize Recipes"
reprinted from the Daily Telegraph

✣ CUMBERLAND RUM BUTTER ✣

*I think myself that you have to have a very sweet tooth to appreci-
ate this famous specialty. The following formula is another from
the* Daily Telegraph *book cited above. Maddeningly, the people
who sent in the recipes collected together in the book are not named,
but the author of this one notes that to be really good it has to be
made with Barbados sugar. (This is the treacly dark brown sugar
to be found at whole-food stores and most good grocer's shops.)*

Butter 4oz, Barbados sugar ¾lb, grated nutmeg ½oz, cinnamon a
good pinch, rum 1 wineglassful.

Cream the warmed butter with the sugar, add the grated nutmeg
and cinnamon. Beat well, then add the rum. Beat again.

Serve in a small glass or China bowl, and sift caster sugar over it.
This is an excellent accompaniment to Christmas pudding.

MINCEMEAT

CHRISTMAS MINCEMEAT and Christmas plum pudding and cake are all such typical examples of the English fondness for spiced fruit mixtures that it seems almost unnecessary to include recipes for them in this little book. It so happens, though, that I have been asked many times for a good mincemeat recipe, so perhaps an interesting one is not all that common.

This is the one I have used for about twenty-five years. It isn't an ancestral one, but came from a lifelong friend, Marian Thomas, who had it, I think, from an aunt who was a notable Westmorland cook.

When Marian passed it on to me she was very insistent that bought shredded suet should not be used. It would prevent the mincemeat from keeping, so she told me. I am afraid that I disobeyed her instructions and used a bought packet of suet. Shredding suet is such a terrible task, I cannot make myself spend so much time and effort on it. The first batch of mincemeat I made using ready-prepared suet kept 5 years. The last jar was a bit dried out. I added more brandy, and it came back to life.

The ingredients are 1½lb of sharp apples, ¾lb of stoneless raisins, ¾lb of currants, ¼lb of mixed peel, ¾lb of sultanas, ¾lb of suet, 2oz of skinned and coarsely chopped almonds, ½ teaspoon each of grated nutmeg, cinnamon and mace, ¾lb of sugar, rind and juice of 1 lemon and 1 orange, 5 tablespoons of brandy or rum.

Wash and dry all fruit. Chop the peeled and carefully cored apples. Mix all ingredients well together, adding brandy last.

Fill stoneware jars and tie them down with thick grease-proof paper, or alternatively pack the mincemeat into glass preserving jars with screw or clip-on tops. This amount makes approximately 6lb of mincemeat.

Notes

1. One of the vital points about making mincemeat for storage is to make quite sure that no scrap of bruised or brown apple flesh finds its way into the mixture.

2. Do remember that mincemeat must be stored in a dry, airy place, not in a kitchen, not, of course, in a damp cellar, and not in any room that is excessively heated. I have taken to keeping mine in a boxroom, not heated at all, where I also store pumpkins for the winter.

✦ MINCED PYES ✦

This recipe, which must date from the early nineteenth century, comes from Lady Sysonby's Cook Book, *first published in 1935. Lady Sysonby says that it is her great-grandmother's recipe.*

Of apples, suet, and currants each 1lb; raisins and sugar ½lb; candied orange and lemon of each 1½oz; ¼oz of salt; of cinnamon and mace each 1½oz and ¼oz respectively; ¼ pint of red wine; 1 glass French brandy and mix all well together.

✦ EXCELLENT MINCEMEAT ✦

I have a serious grouch against the publishers of the centenary edition of Mrs. Beeton for not having thought to include in their

*new publication any single one of the recipes actually written by
the young woman whose name has been selling their cookery
books for more than 100 years. Here is one of Mrs. Beeton's own
mincemeat recipes, from the original 1861*
Household Management.

Ingredients: 3 large lemons, 3 large apples, 1lb of stoned raisins, 1lb of currants, 1lb of suet, 2lb of moist sugar, 1oz of sliced candied citron, 1oz of sliced candied orange peel, and the same quantity of lemon peel, 1 teacupful of brandy, 2 tablespoons of orange marmalade.

Mode: Grate the rinds of the lemons; squeeze out the juice, strain it and boil the remainder of the lemons until tender enough to pulp or chop very finely. Then add to this pulp the apples, which should be baked, and their skins and cores removed; put in the remaining ingredients one by one, and, as they are added, mix everything very thoroughly together.

Put the mincemeat into a stone jar with a closely-fitting lid, and in a fortnight it will be ready for use.

Seasonable: This should be made the first or second week in December.

↬ THE GOOD DAUGHTER'S MINCEMEAT PUDDING ↫
*This is Eliza Acton's own way of dealing with mince pies.
The recipe is sub-titled Author's Receipt. It may come in
handy for those who don't want to make pastry.*

Lay into a rather deep tart dish some thin slices of French roll very slightly spread with butter and covered with a thick layer of mincemeat; place a second tier lightly on these, covered in the same way with the mincemeat; then pour gently in a custard made with three well-whisked eggs, three-quarter of a pint of new milk or thin cream, the slightest pinch of salt, and two ounces of sugar. Let the pudding stand to soak for an hour, then bake it gently until it is quite firm in the center, this will be in from three-quarters of an hour to a full hour.

ELIZA ACTON
Modern Cookery, 1845

✦ LEMON OR ORANGE MINCE PIES ✦

Squeeze the juice of a large lemon or Seville orange. Boil the outside till it will completely mash. Chop fine, and add to the three or four apples, a quarter pound each of suet and sugar, half a pound of currants; two ounces of candied peel, and the juice. If not quite moist enough, add a little white wine. Bake in a short crust.

ESTHER COPLEY
The Housekeeper's Guide, 1834

✦ ESTHER COPLEY'S SHORT CRUST ✦
FOR LEMON MINCE PIES

Rub to a cream three ounces of butter, add to it one pound of flour well dried, and two ounces of loaf sugar; rub them well together; then add the yolks of two eggs and as much cream boiling hot as will bring it to a proper consistence; roll it thin, and bake in a moderate oven. If a richer paste be desired the quantity of butter may be increased.

ESTHER COPLEY
The Housekeeper's Guide, 1834

CREAMS AND CAKES

⤳ CRÈME FORESTIÈRE ⬳

*Ceremonially burning plum pudding, ritual mince pies, almonds,
raisins, walnuts, tangerines, sugar-plums in wooden boxes, fat
marrons glacés surrounded by crackling paper frills — such warm
winter charm has the traditional Christmas dessert that further
ideas upon the subject seem unnecessary, any extra burden upon the
cook an imposition, were it not that the season is dedicated to hospitality, and that children take such intense pleasure in sweet things.
Consider then some of these Christmas dessert delicacies: caramelized
oranges, decorative, surprising, and easy on already full stomachs;
little bonbons of chocolate or chestnuts, which look pretty on the
table and are fun to make; and an Italian chocolate torrone (see
"Torrone Molle," below) will, I could almost guarantee it, become
the love of any household where there are children. All these dishes
are simple enough in preparation, and more than considerate of the
cook's time — as is this extravagant cream made of Kirsch and eggs.*

The author of this recipe, Auricoste de Lazarque, named it
crème forestière *after an inspector of forestry in Lorraine who
first introduced him to it. This inspector claimed that the ingredients
could always be found in the smallest village (perhaps, in Lorraine,
in 1909) and recommended it to the notice of sportsmen, soldiers
on the march, and country-house hostesses faced
with unexpected guests.*

Break 2 yolks of egg into a bowl, stir them for several minutes
with a wooden spoon, always in the same direction. Incorpo-
rate gradually 2 teaspoonfuls of sugar and 2 of Kirsch. One by
one, add 3 or 4 more yolks of egg, allowing for each egg 2 more

teaspoonfuls each of Kirsch and sugar. Continue to stir, as for a mayonnaise, until you have a smooth and thick cream. Serve it in small pots, quickly, before the strength of the Kirsch has had time to evaporate. The quantities given will fill 4 little egg ramekins.

↠ ATHOLL BROSE ↞

There are numerous variations of this Highland whisky and honey and cream mixture. Some are liquid enough to drink, some are eaten with a spoon. The whisky content is also very variable. The following formula is the spoon version. It is Eleanor Jenkinson's, one her niece described to me as being always served at family music parties (see "The Pudding," above). It is rich, delicious, expensive, but provided you have the ingredients to hand, mixed in the twinkling of an eye. The formula is also an easy one to memorize.

"Two parts of honey, one of whisky, six of cream. Mix the honey and whisky together in a bowl, add the cream, stir it and ladle into wine glasses."

Miss Jenkinson added: "It makes a very good sweet, served in custard glasses, with a spoonful of whipped cream on the top."

Notes

1. Interpreted in tablespoons, 2 of honey, 1 of whisky, 6 of cream, the yield is enough for 1 largish wineglass. I don't think one could manage much more. Personally I find it a little over-sweet, and so reduce the honey by half. Measuring honey in tablespoons is always tricky, and the amount tends to get over-done.

2. The whisky I use is Glenfiddich or whatever pure malt I may have. An extravagance, and some would say an unsuitable way to treat a

luxury product. But as a non-spirit drinker, I find pure malt one of the few I can take. Use a more everyday whisky if that is what you have to hand.

3. I don't think the extra whipped cream on top is a good idea. To me a little thin pouring cream is preferable. But then I start off with rich Jersey cream.

4. If you make your own yogurt, try using it instead of cream. Provided it's fresh, it's delicious, and it won't separate. But shop yogurt is too acid.

✣ Torrone Molle (Uncooked Chocolate Cake) ✣

This gorgeous invention needs barely a couple of minutes actual cooking and the rest of the preparation is of the utmost simplicity. The word torrone *is Italian for all kinds of nougat, and* molle *means soft. In this recipe, which came well over thirty years ago from a Tuscan cook called Lina, the soft nougat is molded in a tin and turned out when well chilled.*

Ingredients are 6oz each of unsweetened cocoa, butter, ground almonds, sugar, and plain *Petit Beurre* biscuits; 1 whole egg and 1 yolk; a little sweet almond oil for the tin. I give this recipe in rather smaller quantities than that in which Lina used to make it. She had a number of fussy grown-ups and an appreciative schoolboy to feed; but it is rather an extravagant cake to make on a large scale.

Work the cocoa and butter together until you have a soft paste. Stir in the ground almonds. In a thick saucepan melt the sugar, moistened with a little water, over gentle heat. Add the cocoa mixture. Beat in the whole egg and the yolk. Now break the biscuits into pieces about the size of almonds. Stir or fold these into the soft nougat preparation. This last operation has to be performed gently so that the biscuits don't crumble. The idea is that when the *torrone molle* is finally turned out and cut, the little pieces of biscuit should look like whole almonds studding the chocolate mass.

Have ready either a turban mould or a simple loaf tin of 1¾ pint capacity, brushed with sweet almond oil. Turn your prepared *torrone* into the tin, smooth it well down, cover it with a piece of foil or oiled parchment and leave it in the refrigerator until well chilled, preferably overnight. It should then turn out easily.

I published this recipe in *Italian Food* in 1954, and it has since been a good deal adapted in various ways. Some cooks think it's a good idea to add a spoonful or two of rum or whisky, others add a little black coffee, others again a few drops of bitter almond essence. I'm not sure if any of these additions are real improvements, but if you choose to try one or other of them, be very careful not to overdo either the liquid content or the flavoring.

✦ CHOCOLATE ICE CREAM ✦

This recipe is one I published in Vogue House and Garden *in July 1959. That year my sister decided to give it a try at Christmas. Her children were reaching the stage where ice creams were the great treat. The chocolate one was so well received that thereafter there was no going back. She made it year after year, in ever increasing quantities, freezing it in the ice compartment of her huge refrigerator.*

For a generous pint of ice cream you need the yolks of 3 large eggs, 3oz of white sugar, I pint of single cream, or half and half double cream and milk, 4oz of bitter chocolate, 2 tablespoons of black coffee or rum or whisky or plain water.

Beat the yolks with the sugar, whisk them with the cream and milk, or whirl them all in the blender for a few seconds. Cook them to a thin custard, in a heavy saucepan over very low heat, stirring constantly. If you feel safer with a double saucepan then use one. I don't because I find it so slow, but for a large quantity I cook the custard in a bowl which fits inside a very deep saucepan of gently simmering water. If the worst happens and the custard develops lumps, quickly return it to the blender and give it another whirl. This should cure the trouble.

When the custard is ready – it needn't, and indeed shouldn't, be very thick – remove the saucepan from the heat and prepare the chocolate. All you have to do is break it up, put it in a fireproof plate or bowl with the coffee, rum, whisky or water, let it melt in a slow oven. Stir it smooth, transfer it to a big bowl, pour the hot custard over it, gradually, stirring until you have a thin but smooth cream. Transfer it to the refrigerator and leave until perfectly cold. By that time it will have thickened. Give it another whirl in the blender, and transfer it quickly to a mould, tin, or other container, cover it and freeze at once.

About an hour before you need it, transfer the frozen cream from the freezer to the refrigerator. To turn it out, stand the container for a couple of minutes in a bigger one containing just a little cold water, or wrap a cloth wrung out in cold water all round it. Either of these methods works much better than standing the container in hot water, as more generally advised.

I like plain unsweetened unadorned pouring cream with a chocolate ice, and something very simple in the way of a biscuit. For years I always had Romary's beautiful thin wheaten biscuits with this chocolate ice, but these have now vanished. Fingers of shortbread are an alternative.

Notes

1. Good bitter chocolate with a high percentage of cocoa butter is expensive, which makes chocolate ice cream something of a luxury. The trouble with inferior brands of chocolate is that the cocoa from which they are made has been divested of most of its own cocoa butter, which is replaced with some much poorer fat, affecting the thickening and setting properties of the chocolate as well as its flavor. To help counteract the defect, 1oz of unsalted butter can be blended with the chocolate while it is hot from the melting process and before the custard is added.

2. When increasing the amounts, it isn't necessary to multiply everything by three or four. For example, if you start out with 12oz of chocolate, the proportions of sugar, eggs, milk and cream should be increased by not more than two and a half times, say 7oz of sugar, 1½ pints of milk, ½ pint of cream, and 7 or 8 egg yolks.

3. With chocolate, ginger is a particularly good combination of flavors. If you have a jar of ginger in syrup, or some dry crystallized ginger, try adding a little, chopped small, to the ice cream mixture just before you put it into the freezer.

4. This chocolate ice can also be made in an ice-cream machine, following the manufacturer's instructions. JN

→ GINGER CREAM ←

A recipe adapted from a much more elaborate one given by John Simpson; it provides a useful way of using some of the ginger in syrup that one gets given at Christmas time.

Ingredients are a strip of lemon peel, a sprinkling of cinnamon and nutmeg, 1 pint of single cream, 5-6 egg yolks, 3 or 4 tablespoons of sugar, 2 tablespoons each of ginger syrup and the ginger itself, finely chopped. Put the lemon peel and the spices into the cream and bring it to the boil. Beat the yolks of the eggs very thoroughly with the sugar. Pour the hot cream into the egg mixture, stir well, return to the saucepan and cook gently, as for a custard, until the mixture has thickened. Take the pan from the fire, extract the lemon peel, go on stirring until the cream is cool. Add the syrup and the chopped ginger.

Leave it in the refrigerator overnight, then, stirring well so that the ginger does not sink to the bottom, pour into little custard glasses, small wineglasses or coffee cups. There will be enough to fill eight glasses.

If you subtract ¼ pint of cream from the original mixture, adding the same quantity of whipped double cream when the custard is quite cold, and freeze it in the foil-covered ice-trays of the refrigerator (at maximum freezing point) for 2 hours, this makes a very attractive ice cream.

→ A CHRISTMAS RECIPE FOR ←
AN OLD TESTAMENT CAKE

4½ cups of 1 Kings IV 22
1½ lb of Judges V 25
2 cups of Jeremiah VI 20
2 cups of 1 Sam. XXX 12
2 cups of Numbers XVII 8
2 cups of Nahum III 12
2 teaspoons of 1 Sam. XIV 25
Season to taste with 2 Chron. IX 9
Six Jeremiah XVII 11

1½ cups of Judges IV 19
2 teaspoons of Amos IV 5
A pinch of Leviticus II 13
Directions Proverbs XXIII 14
Bake 1 to 2 hours.

SOLUTION: *Operative words in each verse:*
Fine flour, Butter, Sweet cane, Raisins, Almonds, Ripe figs,
Honey, Spice, Eggs, Milk, Leaven, Salt, Beat

Note
I found this recipe in Elizabeth's file of other people's work to be used in her Christmas book. Exceptionally, she does not give the source. JN

✣ CHESTNUT AND CHOCOLATE CAKE ✣
An excellent and comparatively simple chestnut sweet that is half pudding, half cake.

Shell and skin 1lb of chestnuts. Cover them with half milk and half water and simmer them very gently until they are very soft, which will take about an hour. Drain off the liquid. Sieve the chestnuts. To the resulting purée add a syrup made from 3oz of white sugar and 2 or 3 tablespoons of water, then beat in 2oz of softened butter. When this mixture is thoroughly amalgamated, turn it into a rectangular mould of ¾-1 pint capacity. (An ice-tray from the refrigerator is a good substitute if you have no small loaf tin.) This should first be very lightly brushed with oil. Leave until next day in the refrigerator or larder. To turn it out, run a knife round the edges and ease out the cake.

Cover it with the following mixture: Break up 3oz of plain chocolate and melt it on a fireproof plate in a cool oven with

4 or 5 lumps of sugar and 2 or 3 tablespoons of water. Stir it smooth; add 1oz of butter. Let it cool a little, then with a palette knife cover the whole cake with the chocolate, smoothing it with a knife dipped in water. Leave it to set before serving. Ample for four.

→ APPLE AND ALMOND CAKE ←

Here is a nice pudding made of real ingredients that makes a very charming pudding for children. It is also, I am sure, very wholesome; at any rate, it has a lovely refreshing flavor.

3lb of crisp eating apples, ¾–1lb of sugar, rind of 1 lemon, ½ pint of thick cream, 1½oz of whole almonds.

Pare and core the apples. Put the peel and cores in a saucepan and just cover them with water. Simmer for about 30 minutes, strain the juice into a wide pan. Stir in the sugar and the thinly sliced apples. Add the lemon rind. Cook for about half an hour until the juice will set like jelly; the apple slices should still be whole, not broken to a pulp. Turn into an oblong loaf tin (about 2 pint capacity), press well down; leave until next day.

Turn out on to a long dish and cover the cake with slightly sweetened and very lightly whipped cream, then stud it all over with the skinned, split, and lightly roasted almonds. This should be enough for 6-8.

→ ORANGE AND ALMOND CAKE ←

2oz of fine bread crumbs, the juice of 3 oranges, grated rind of 1 orange, 4oz of ground almonds, orange-flower water, 4 eggs, 4oz of sugar, ½ teaspoon of salt, cream.

Mix together the bread crumbs, orange juice and grated

orange rind, add the ground almonds, and, if available, a tablespoon of orange-flower water.

Beat the egg yolks with the sugar and salt until almost white. Add to the first mixture. Fold in the stiffly beaten egg whites. Pour into a square cake tin, buttered and sprinkled with bread crumbs, and bake in a moderate oven, 350°F, for about 40 minutes.

When cold turn the cake out and cover the top with whipped cream (about ¼ pint). Very good and light, and excellent for a sweet at luncheon or dinner.

✣ GALETTE BRESSANE ✣

The galette à la boulangère in Escoffier's farmhouse Christmas menu (see "Christmas in France") would have been a yeast-leavened confection, its precise form depending on the local tradition. Escoffier didn't reveal where the dinner had taken place, so I suggest here the galette invariably offered by the late Mère Brazier at her lovely restaurant at the Col de la Luère above Lyon. Her galette was much like a brioche in composition, although not in shape. It was very simple and of great finesse.

Ingredients are 1 level teaspoon of dried yeast, just under ¼ pint of tepid milk, ½ lb of plain flour, 5oz of caster sugar, ½ level teaspoon of salt, 3 whole eggs, 6oz of butter.

Mix the yeast and tepid milk in a cup. Sift the flour into a mixing bowl, add the sugar and the salt. Break in the eggs, then the yeast and milk. Amalgamate all ingredients, then work in the softened butter, beating very vigorously until the mixture starts to become elastic. Mère Brazier's recipe says 15 minutes; I don't find it necessary to go on quite so long, but then I am using only half the quantities given in her recipe – originally she was probably allowing for several galettes.

Cover the dough – or rather batter – with a sheet of polythene and leave it in a warm place until it has risen and is very light – about 2 hours. Beat it down thoroughly, cover it again and leave it, this time in a cold place but not the refrigerator. When you are ready to cook the galette, work the dough again very thoroughly.

Turn it into a buttered cake tin, of 2½ pint capacity (I use a non-stick tin for this kind of cake). It should be only half full. Cover it and leave to rise once more. It will take 2½ -3 hours to rise nearly to the top of the tin.

Heat the oven to 425°F.

Scatter a few little pieces of butter and a tablespoon or two of caster sugar over the top of the cake. Bake it in the center of the oven for 15 minutes, and for another 15 minutes with the heat lowered to 375°F. If you have an ovenproof earthenware bowl, it is a very good idea to invert it over the galette; the initial baking time will then be 30 minutes under the bowl, and a further 10 minutes uncovered at the lower temperature. The baking-under system makes the dough rise better and produces a better crust. It is a marvelous method of cooking all yeast doughs and bread. But the bowl gets very hot, so be sure to handle it with thick oven gloves.

Leave the galette in its tin for about 10 minutes before attempting to turn it out.

If you don't want to serve the cake with an ice cream – Mère Brazier's was a beautiful vanilla one with a hot chocolate sauce – it is just as delicious with many other desserts, such as soft white fresh cream cheese with fresh cream, or any cooked fruit dish, or just by itself with a glass of Beaumes de Venise.

PERSIMMONS ARE perhaps the most delicious and beautiful of the imported fruits of the Christmas season. It is only in recent years that they have been appearing in any quantity in our shops, so I quote the following splendid description of them.

The one other fruit I know that can be eaten only when it has gone soft and has "bletted" is the persimmon, that beautiful "golden apple," which should clearly have hailed from the gardens of the Hesperides. In point of fact it hails from Japan (Diospyros kaki) and the Southern States of the United States (Diospyros virginiana). Is it not strange that flesh which in both cases, until that stage is reached, is so harsh and wryly astringent as to be utterly uneatable should thereafter be transmuted into substances so agreeable to the taste?

The persimmon tree is of a large and noble growth – with the mulberry it is among the tallest fruit-trees in the world – and in the European summer the "plums" (for that is what they look like), still of a pale apricot hue, gleam coldly luminous among the leaves. The trees are certainly handsome enough at this season of the year in their natural beauty; but in late November and in December, when the fruit has ripened into edibility, they assume the tinge of another kind of beauty: the boughs, now entirely stripped of leaves, are weighed down under their burden of fruit, by this time no longer just a pale reflection of lunar austerity but richly, warmly glowing – great balls of orange-brown amber – against the sharp clear blue of the Italian winter sky. They look like toy trees – if anything so large may be likened to a toy – to whose naked branches the children of a race of giants have tied the golden globes for a Christmas party in Brobdingnag.

SIR HARRY LUKE, The Tenth Muse

London, Putnam, 1962

Apricots An apricot tasting, that's what I would like to have for Christmas. I love apricots, I love them nearly as much as figs. Figs turn into something quite different when they are dried or preserved, something attractive and often delicious. The dried figs of Bari, packed in boxes with sprigs of fennel and bay leaves, are uniquely dark and soft; dried figs of Portugal come flattened out, with a roasted taste and with almonds stuck round the edges. A friend once brought me Spanish dried figs from his own farm in the hills above Valencia, they were tiny and sugary and almost black. Figs from Korini in Greece are soft as cake and nutmeg-colored; figs from Cyprus, threaded on raffia strings, are rather toffeeish and tough and are good baked in wine flavored with orange or tangerine peel. Figs in tins from Israel are one of the best of such fruits. Crystallized figs from northern Italy and Provence are immensely beguiling in appearance but little flavor survives the boiling and sugaring process.

No preserved fig of any kind that I know bears any resemblance to the fresh fruit. Apricots are different. Dried apricots become more apricotter than fresh ones.

When fresh apricots are in season, all that is necessary is to wash them, make an incision, with a fruit knife, along the natural division of the fruit; arrange the apricots pyramid-wise in a baking dish, add sugar (about ¼lb to 1lb of apricots), a glass of sherry and an equal quantity of water. They will need a good hour's cooking, uncovered, in a moderate oven. Serve them at once. They should be quite soft without being mushy, and here and there the sugar just beginning to caramelize.

Thin cream can go with the apricots, whether they are dried or fresh; the French unsalted double cream cheeses called Isigny or Chambourcy are even better than cream.

⇥ APRICOT ICE CREAM ⇤

1¼lb of ripe apricots, 8fl oz of water, 3oz of sugar, the juice of half a large lemon, ½ pint of double cream. Optionally, 2 or 3 tablespoons of apricot brandy.

Wipe the apricots with a soft cloth, put them in an oven-proof dish with the water. No sugar at this stage. Cover the pot. Cook in a low oven, 325°F, for about 35 minutes or until the apricots are soft. When cool, strain off the juice into a saucepan. Add the sugar and boil to a thin syrup.

Stone the apricots, keeping aside a few of the stones. Purée the fruit. Pour the cooled syrup into the purée. Add the lemon juice. Crack 3 or 4 apricot stones, extract the kernels and crush them to a paste. Stir this into the purée, then press the purée through a fine stainless steel wire or nylon sieve. Chill it thoroughly in the refrigerator.

Before freezing, taste for sweetness, adding more lemon juice if necessary. Turn into a metal or plastic container of about 1¾ pint capacity and transfer to the freezer.

After 2½ hours or so, turn the half-frozen ice into the food processor or high-power blender or beater and beat it until the ice crystals have disappeared. If you have no suitable electric machine, use a big bowl and a heavy whisk or fork. Add the cream and the apricot brandy, and taste again for sweetness. Repack the cream into the container and return to the freezer.

In approximately 3 hours the ice should be frozen to about the right consistency for serving. An extra refinement is to give the ice a second rapid breakdown in the blender or food processor a short while before serving. This restores the thick creamy texture of a good ice cream, and it can now be turned into a dish ready for serving and returned to the freezer for a quarter of an hour. Alternatively, the second breakdown can be performed while the ice cream is still only two-thirds frozen. It is then turned into a simple or fancy mould and returned to the freezer until set.

Notes

1. To crack the apricot stones I find that an ancient, common, metal nutcracker of the most basic design is also the most effective.
2. An alternative to using the apricot kernels is to crush up one or two Italian amaretti di Saronno, the little macaroons wrapped in crackly tissue paper, which are in fact made with apricot kernels, not with bitter almonds as was generally assumed until the listing of ingredients in packed confectionery became compulsory.
3. Most people who make ice cream regularly now have an ice-cream maker. Elizabeth's ices can be made successfully in a machine, following the manufacturer's instructions. However, her instructions for how to freeze ices in trays work well, and the "extra refinement" of a second breakdown in the blender is worthwhile. JN

✦ ICED APRICOT SOUFFLÉ ✦
An iced soufflé or mousse neither cloying nor rubbery, neither pasty nor rock hard but creamy, light and with just enough gelatin to make it set and hold its shape, is quite a rarity. It isn't difficult, but you have to be generous with the cream and sparing with the gelatin. And personally, I find the old-fashioned leaf gelatin more satisfactory than the powdered variety. It is never gluey either in taste or consistency. This method for an iced soufflé or mousse, once mas-

tered, can be applied in principle to all kinds of fruit and also to savory things such as ham, tongue and chicken, and fish.

½lb of fresh apricots, 2oz of sugar, ¼ pint of water, 3 leaves of gelatin, ½ pint of thick cream, the whites of 4 large eggs.

Stew the apricots with the sugar and water until quite soft. Drain off the juice and reserve it. Stone and sieve the fruit, or pulp it in the blender. Cut the gelatin leaves into small pieces, put them into the top half of a double saucepan with the reserved juice and steam over hot water until melted. Strain into the fruit pulp. Fold in the lightly whipped cream, put into the refrigerator until chilled and just beginning to set.

At this stage whip the whites of the eggs until they stand in peaks and fold into the fruit and cream. Turn the mixture into a soufflé dish and pile it high up over the top of the dish so that it looks as if it were about to topple over. But it won't. Return it to the refrigerator to set. An alternative method is to put it in little glass custard cups, one for each person. It will fill 6-8 of these.

To make the soufflé with dried apricots, soak 2oz of dried apricots overnight in water just to cover. Cook them slowly until they are quite soft. Strain them, reserving ¼ pint of the juice. To the pulp add 2oz of sugar and the juice of half a lemon.

Cut the gelatin leaves into small pieces and dissolve them in the reserved juice as described above, and follow the rest of the recipe for fresh apricot soufflé.

✣ MANDARINES GIVRÉES ✣

These frosted tangerines are really hollowed-out tangerines filled with an orange or tangerine ice. They figure often in French festive menus. Escoffier served them at the Carlton in his Christmas menu

for the year 1913. They came as a sorbet in the middle of the meal.
I have never been able to keep enough tangerines in the house at
one time to make a tangerine ice. Tangerines are fruit which have
so enticing a scent, so direct an allure with their skins so easily
shucked off, their little segments so fat with juice and flavor that a
whole tall pyramid of them disappears almost as soon as it has been
arranged in the dish. When one day I again spend my Christmas
in a country where tangerines can be picked from the tree I shall
make tangerine ice according to a beautiful recipe given by Miss
Marjorie Kinnan Rawlings, author of The Yearling *and* Cross
Creek *and a most beguiling writer about the food of Florida*
where she lived, wrote, and taught an assortment of erratic,
temperamental and sometimes illiterate cooks.

This is a Cross Creek spécialité de la maison. Friends cry for it. It is to
my winter what mango ice cream is to the summer. It has an extremely
exotic flavor and is a gorgeous color. Actually, it is very simple, and the
only tricks to it are in having one's own tangerine tree – and the patience
to squeeze the juice from at least a twelve quart bucket of the tangerines.
In the days when black 'Geechee lived with me, it was always her choice
for desserts, knowing its popularity. We usually had a crowd and
served a buffet, and 'Geechee would race through the farmhouse, cap
awry, bearing a loaded tray, and shouting at the top of her strong
lungs, "Tangerine Sherbet comin' up! Sherbet comin' up!"

> Five oz sugar
> Good half pint water
> Grated rind of four tangerines
> One and a half pints tangerine juice
> Juice of one or two lemons

Boil sugar and water ten minutes. Add the grated tangerine rind to
syrup while still hot. Let cool slightly and add tangerine juice and

lemon juice. *Taste for sweetness and acidity, as the tangerines vary. Chill thoroughly, strain and freeze.*
The Marjorie Kinnan Rawlings Cookbook, 1942

⤙ SPICED PRUNES ⤚

To make this excellent and useful dessert it is essential to use whole spices. Ground ones won't do at all.

For 1lb of large prunes the spices needed are: two 2 inch pieces of cinnamon or cassia bark, 2 level teaspoons of coriander seeds, 2 blades of mace, 4 whole cloves.

Put the prunes and spices in a bowl or earthenware casserole. Just cover them with cold water. Leave overnight. Next day cook the prunes, in an uncovered casserole, in a low oven or over very moderate direct heat until they are swollen but not mushy. About half the cooking water will have evaporated. Take out the fruit and remove the stones.

Heat up the remaining juice with the spices, until it is slightly syrupy. Pour it through a strainer over the prunes.

To be eaten cold, with cream or yogurt, or with the variation of Sweet-Sour Cabbage in the "Vegetables" chapter.

Notes

1. *Cassia is a variant of cinnamon. The two are very easily distinguished. Cinnamon quills are long, smooth and curled, cassia bark is rough and comes in large chips. Although often held to be inferior to cinnamon there are those – among them some Pakistani cooks – who consider cassia the better of the two. It is indeed cassia bark that appears to be most often used in tandoori restaurant cooking, at any rate in London. Confusion arises, however, because Pakistani spice sellers and cooks insist that cassia bark is cinnamon.*
2. *Mace is the beautiful orange lacy covering of the nutmeg. When*

dried it turns pale tawny in color and is very hard. It is marketed in broken pieces called blades. These give out a wonderful aroma when cooking. Unfortunately, most people buy mace in powder form and so have no notion whatever of its true character. In this dish of spiced prunes there is no substitute for whole mace.

3. An alternative way of using spiced prunes is to leave them in the turned-out oven after they are cooked. By the time the oven is cold, the prunes have soaked up nearly all the juice. They are fat and swollen. Serve them just as they are, without stoning them, as an after-dinner sweetmeat.

↛ Buttered Apples ↚

For this elementary but beautifully scented dish, so good with a glass of rich white wine, you need 2lb of good, sweet, crisp dessert apples, and the other ingredients are 2oz of unsalted butter and 3 or 4 tablespoons of white sugar, a vanilla pod.

Peel, quarter and core the apples, then slice them thinly. Heat the butter in a large wide frying-pan. Put in the apples, add the sugar (if you have vanilla sugar so much the better; or add a vanilla pod which is removed before serving). Cook gently until the apples are pale golden and transparent. Turn the slices over very carefully, so as not to break them, and if they are very closely packed in the pan, shake it so that the layer at the bottom does not stick. Serve them hot. Cream is not really necessary, it spoils the exquisite scent and flavor of the butter and apple mixture. But if you like to produce a more spectacular dish, then you can warm a glass of Calvados in a tiny pan or a ladle, and pour it flaming over the apples as you bring them to table in the pan in which they have cooked. Enough for three.

✦ VANILLA SUGAR ✦

Put a vanilla pod in a jar filled up with caster sugar. After a few days the sugar will be delicately flavored with the true vanilla taste.

✦ DIANA'S APPLES ✦
A new version of an old recipe, much liked by children.

Peel and core 2lb of semi-sweet apples. Slice them, put them in a fireproof pot with 2 tablespoons of water. Cook them, covered, in a medium oven, 350°F, for about 30 minutes, or until they are quite soft. Mash them to a purée. Sweeten this with 3 or 4 tablespoons of honey. Turn into a shallow serving dish. Sprinkle the top with grated bitter chocolate spiced with a little powdered cinnamon.

Cinnamon-flavored chocolate stems from the sixteenth century when chocolate was first brought to Spain from South America. By the second half of the seventeenth century the chocolate-drinking habit had spread to France and Italy and England. Cinnamon was the flavoring habitually used. In Mexico it still is, and in just one of the half dozen chocolate factories in the market town of Villajoyosa in south-eastern Spain cinnamon-flavored chocolate is still being produced.

Note
Diana was Elizabeth's sister, for whose family of five children Elizabeth prepared Christmas meals for many years. Their Christmas celebrations are described in "Cooking for a Family." JN

→ Pears Baked in Wine (or Cider) ←
*A method of making the most intractable of cooking pears
very delicious. It is especially suitable for those households
where there is a solid fuel cooker.*

Peel the pears, leaving the stalks on. Put them in a tall fire-proof dish or earthenware crock. Add about 3oz of sugar per 1lb of pears. Half cover with red table wine, sweet dessert wine, or medium-sweet cider. Fill to the top with water. Bake in a very slow oven, 150°F, for anything between 5 and 7 hours, or even all night, until the pears are quite tender.

These pears, depending on the cooking liquid deep rich red or amber gold by the time they are cooked, are served cold in their remaining juice (it can be thickened to a syrup by a few minutes fast boiling), with cream or creamed rice separately. The best way to arrange them is in a pyramid, stalk uppermost, in a shallow bowl.

Quinces cooked in the same way, but with rather more sugar, are equally delicious and even more beautiful.

→ Pears Baked in Red Wine ←
*This is a dish rather different from the old favorite given
above, in that in this recipe the fruit is not peeled. Initial
preparations are therefore minimal.*

Conference or Bon Chrétien pears are put whole into a casserole and covered in half red wine and half water with the addition of a tablespoon of sugar per 1lb of pears.

Cook, covered, in a low oven, 300°F, for about 2 hours. Remove the pears to a dish. Reduce the wine to the consistency of a syrup.

Serve hot or cold, strewn with white candy sugar crushed in a mortar. The skins of the pears (unlike the skins of baked apples) can be eaten and give the fruit a most delicious flavor and beautiful appearance.

✦ SUGARED ORANGES ✦

Halve and quarter the oranges, scoop the flesh from the pith and skin with a serrated knife and, adding white sugar, store the orange segments in a wide covered glass jar in the refrigerator, adding to them whenever you have a moment to prepare a few extra.

At Christmas dinner, and at the meals to follow, a lot of people are quite enormously grateful for the clean, fresh taste of sliced oranges instead of the cloying heaviness of the pudding or the mince pies.

Serve the oranges, chilled, in deep wineglasses. According to the size of the oranges allow 1, 1½ or 2 per person and, if you like, pour a tablespoon of Kirsch or Cointreau into each glass just before the meal, or perhaps a little lemon juice and a sprinkling of freshly chopped mint leaves.

If you make the quick version of Cumberland sauce (see "Sauces, Pickles and Chutney") this is a good way to use the flesh of the oranges.

FRUMENTY OR FERMITY

THIS SPLENDID INVENTION, a mixture of whole wheat grains boiled to a jelly and then enriched with milk, cream, eggs and spices, goes back a long way in our cookery tradition, almost certainly as far back as the Roman occupation – the name derives from the Latin *frumentum,* wheat or corn – possibly even to far more ancient times. All wheat-growing countries have, or had, the equivalent of frumenty, and probably from the earliest days of wheat cultivation some form of porridge was made by boiling the cleaned grains in water.

What happens once the grains burst and the substance we know as starch is freed, is that the whole mass sets to a thick jelly in which the softened husks of the grain are embedded. This made a highly nutritious and sustaining brew, all the more attractive in that it was soft and easy to eat, whereas mastication of the bread or flat hearth cakes of early days, full of unground particles of husk and grit from the primitive grinding stones, cracked, broke, or wore down the teeth. Wheat, however, was a luxury and not for every day. Boiling it for a pottage or porridge was extravagant, so frumenty came to be regarded as a special preparation for the celebration of religious festivals and holidays.

By medieval times frumenty had become a feast dish for the rich. Cooks added milk, cream, spices and sometimes eggs. In Mediterranean countries the milk originally came from ewes or goats, as did our own, milch kine being a comparatively late introduction. Then came almond milk, in the days when the Christian church forbade the eating of all animal milk during Lent and on the innumerable fast days throughout the year. In England, almond milk was another luxury. To make it, massive quantities of imported almonds were skinned, pounded to crumbs, steeped in water for a night, then wrung through a cloth. The resulting liquid was usually sweetened, and thereby slightly thickened, with honey, or later, with the great new spice: sugar. On fast days almond milk replaced animal milk in all the cooking of the rich.

By the fourteenth century the royalty and nobles of England and France had come to regard frumenty or *fromentée* as the necessary accompaniment of venison and of the porpoise which was its fasting day substitute. Few banquets or ceremonial feasts were complete without one or other of the two combinations. To us they sound so strange as to be barely credible. But possibly the soothing nature of the frumenty went some way to tame the violent flavors of the game, whether of land or sea. It has to be remembered too that at this period everything was eaten with the fingers or with a spoon, so probably the gobbets of venison or porpoise would have been stirred into bowls of frumenty, and all eaten as one complete dish. To enliven its appearance the frumenty was often colored with saffron. They loved colored food, those medieval magnates and princes of the church. Indeed they loved all brightly colored things, and yellow was the grandest of all, the royal color, the color of gold.

While their lords and masters feasted upon ton after ton of spiced meat and game, sea- and fresh-water fish, chicken and almond *blancmangers*, sweetmeats, colored jellies, fine white wheaten loaves and the choicest white wheat grains boiled for frumenty, the men and women who toiled for them had to make do with a spare diet of coarse vegetables, kale and field peas, cabbage, leeks and onions, broths thickened with oatmeal or barley, salt fish, the occasional hunk of pork or bacon, fresh curd cheese, milk and eggs and rough brown bread made from mixtures of rye meal and wheat bran or barley and oatmeal. To them a dish of frumenty made from good wheat was for special days only, Christmas, Easter, and mid-Lent Sunday. Gradually, frumenty became one of the established festival dishes of country people and at some stage, probably during the seventeenth century, the farmers' wives started preparing the wheat in sufficient quantity to take the surplus to market for sale to the townspeople, who could thus buy their frumenty all but ready for the table, a brief re-cooking in milk, with the addition of cream, spices, and whatever other enrichments they wanted or could afford, being all that was required. This convenient form of take-away food, which saved much labor and fuel, was quite commonly prepared until the end of the nineteenth century, and in some parts of the country even survived the Great War, when wheat became too precious to be used for anything but bread.

When in the early 1930s Florence White was collecting recipes and information for the fine book that eventually became *Good Things in England*, she received letters from correspondents in the West Country, Yorkshire, the Midland counties and Lincolnshire who all had recent memories of the boiled wheat for fermity or frumenty being sold at country markets, in town dairies and by street sellers. One of these correspondents, a Lady Robinson of Whitby in Yorkshire, wrote in 1931 that "frumenty is still eaten on Christmas Eve with cheese and gingerbread in this neighbourhood." Another part of the country where frumenty survived as a Christmas dish was East Anglia. Allan Jobson, the Suffolk writer who has recorded so much valuable information about the old life and customs of his native county, gives the following description of the annual ritual of frumenty preparation as it had probably been practiced by his forebears for generation after generation.

On Christmas Eve the traditional dish of furmentory (frumenty) was prepared. The wheat to be stewed was placed in a long bag, and Charlie and Eliza catching hold at each end, using the bag as a chute, would throw the contents to one another, and beat it, so that the husks came away from the grain. To the prepared wheat was added a thickening of flour, and it was left for the night. At five o'clock the next morning Charlie got up, put the preparation in the boiler, and stirred it for nearly three hours lest it should burn. It was eaten off old wooden platters (heirlooms) at eight o'clock breakfast, sugar, spice and rum being added.

ALLAN JOBSON, *An Hour-Glass on the Run*
Michael Joseph, London, 1959

How sad, and how mistaken, that we have allowed this ancient and much-loved delicacy – for it is truly delicious – to vanish so completely. In Italy its equivalent has survived. Prepared wheat, *grano amollato* or softened grain, can still sometimes be found at a *pizzicheria*, or grocery store, or on a street-market stall in the Rome and Naples regions. In Italy so many services of this kind are – or were – available. In the markets of Tuscany chick peas could be bought ready-soaked for cooking, from huge mottled green and white glazed earthenware bowls. So could beans. And salt cod, also soaked ready for Fridays. Nowadays most of such time-saving commodities have progressed from those beautiful bowls into tins. That goes also for *grano amollato*. Not long ago I bought some tinned frumenty wheat from an Italian grocery in my quarter of Chelsea. Admittedly it is called *gran pastiera*, wheat for the *pastiera napoletana*, and is mostly, I suspect, used for that daunting festive specialty. The *pastiera* is a huge open pie of *pasta frolla*, short pastry enriched with eggs, sugar, butter and lard, the filling being fresh ricotta cheese, plus the boiled wheat re-cooked in milk, candied peel, eggs, sugar, confectioner's custard, spices, orange-flower water. More pastry is arranged in a lattice on the top of the pie. A deadly, although fascinating confection, with its layer upon layer of tastes and textures. I have never tried to make it, and I think I will not start now. I used my tin of *grano amollato* to make frumenty. It was so good and so easy that I pass on the method, and urge anyone who sees a tin of *gran pastiera* at an Italian provision shop to buy it and have a try at frumenty. I think it would be difficult not to see why our ancestors were so charmed by it. To reflect that our nursery rice pudding is certainly one of its descendants is to see that our tastes in food aren't always more subtle than those of our ancestors. Where rice pudding is flaccid and infantile, frumenty has guts and bite, contrast in texture. Nor are we necessarily more alive to nutritional values. I think it was appreciated centuries ago that frumenty is a whole food. The wheat grain, its germ and all its main properties are intact. The sweet and nutty flavor of the grain is enticing, and there is a certain velvety quality about the dish as a whole that makes it difficult to define or to compare with any other food I know.

✦ Frumenty ✦

To make 4–6 small bowls of frumenty, ingredients are: ½lb of prepared wheat (the Italian tins contain approximately 15oz; the unused grain can be stored in the fridge for a few days ready for another batch); 1 pint of creamy milk; 3oz of seedless raisins; ¼ pint of thick cream; a sprinkling of ground cinnamon.

Put the wheat in a heavy saucepan, preferably stainless steel or Teflon-lined. Cover it with the milk. Add the raisins. Cover the pan. If you cook on gas or electricity put the pan on an iron trivet or toasting grid standing over the source of heat. This is important. The milk and wheat mixture catches and sticks easily. The point is stressed in many of the ancient recipes.

Let the wheat and milk cook over very low heat for 15–20 minutes until the whole mixture is creamy but not too solid. Stir in a little of the cream and leave until the next day. By this time the wheat will have swelled again. Stir in the rest of the cream.

To serve the frumenty, spoon it into bowls. It can be eaten hot or cold – I prefer it cold – with the cinnamon sprinkled on at the last moment.

→ Frumenty with Barley ←

To make this frumenty from scratch you need whole barley grains (whole-food shops stock them). With ½ lb you can prepare enough to fill a 3-pint bowl.

Put the washed grains in a deepish pot (there used to be special tall narrow pots for cooking the grain for frumenty) and cover them with 1¾ pints of water. Cook covered in a very moderate oven, 325°F, until the grains are soft and swollen and the water nearly all absorbed. This will take about 3 hours. The basis of the frumenty is now ready. It can be used at once or it can safely be refrigerated for a few days. How many days are a few? Well, say 4 or 5.

For the second part of the preparation you need milk, cream, raisins and cinnamon approximately in the following proportions: for 1lb of cooked barley grains ½ pint of very fresh rich milk, 4–6oz of seedless raisins, ½ pint of cream. The cinnamon you must judge for yourself. Try to have it freshly ground in a coffee grinder and turned into a small sugar caster or flour dredger.

Weigh out the boiled grain (it weighs very heavy; although 1lb doesn't look much, it goes a long way), then follow the previous recipe, but stir frequently during the cooking.

Notes

1. It may be noted that neither salt nor sugar is called for in my recipe. Curiously enough salt doesn't seem necessary, and sweetening is supplied by the raisins. But by all means have both sugar and salt on the table for anyone who feels they are needed.

2. I have also omitted the customary enrichment of eggs. Again, I find the brew rich enough without them. If you like to add them, 3 should be enough for the quantities given. Beat them well and stir them into the frumenty only when you have removed it from the heat.

3. If you like to make the frumenty yellow, as did our forebears, make an infusion with saffron threads and a little hot milk taken from the amount to be used to cook the frumenty. Leave this infusion until the milk is brilliant orange. Strain out the saffron, pour the orange-colored milk into the hot frumenty. As in a Milanese risotto, this gives a lovely pungent aroma to the frumenty as well as color – but not everyone cares for the taste of saffron.

4. Another alternative flavoring for frumenty is almond milk or a couple of ounces of finely ground almonds or hazelnuts.

5. It should be noted that barley does not have the same glutinous properties as wheat, and so does not boil to a jelly but rather to a solid mass. It is not so rich, and absorbs much less milk than wheat. Nevertheless it makes lovely, comforting and very nutritious food.

walnuts

✳ Christmas in a Norfolk Village ✳

Grandmother always excelled herself at the Christmas dinner. First, there was a hot mutton pie, with oyster patties, then a huge goose, one which had gobbled up many a tit-bit to hasten its own demise, with attendant vegetables. Ending up with a lemon pudding, plum porridge, junket, apple fritters. And should there be any room, a mince pie, baked in the old-fashioned coffin-shaped crust (learnt of her mother) to represent the cratch or manger in which the Holy Child was laid. What more would you, save a glass or two of harvest ale laced with gin, and drunk from tall glasses (like old champagne) kept by grandmother in the top part of her corner cupboard. Or, as an especial treat, one of the new sherry wine, the oil of which lingered lovingly on the old cut glasses. Or syllabubs made of whipped cream (whipped until the arm ached) and also served in tall glasses.

ALLAN JOBSON, An Hour-Glass on the Run

✳ Christmas Tea ✳

And then came tea, which was another feast to wait on digestion. Home sweet-pickled ham, wanmill cheese, home-made bread and butter, cakes and rusks, washed down with strong tea (Soochong flavored with Pekoe, costing six shillings a pound) and cream in old Worcester noggins, looking like molten gold. But before tea, as was her daily custom, grandmother would drink a glass of cowslip wine.

ALLAN JOBSON, An Hour-Glass on the Run

Drinks

A FINE LAST-DITCH BUY for one's own or somebody else's drink cupboard is a bottle of Sercial Madeira. Preferable to sherry, I think, for flavoring, and to drink with any consommé. If any is left, it is the most valuable wine for sauces, soups, and all dishes in which the wine is added at the last minute. Its effect is extraordinarily subtle. An example: a tablespoon or two added to chestnuts simmered in stock and to be eaten with pheasant or hare.

An assortment of miniature liqueurs is a present that can give a great deal of pleasure and entertainment to any cook interested in experimenting with new combinations of flavors. For savory dishes it is well known how a few drops of one of the orange liqueurs will help the sauce for a duck; cherry brandy, too; and what Kirsch does for cheese fondues and soufflés and for *choucroute*. Then there is anisette for a dressing to go with prawns or mussels or lobster – this sounds pretty obvious, but try it and see. It gives a little flavor reminiscent of fennel and a faint sweetness which seems altogether right once you have tasted it. Don't overdo it, though. A teaspoon to a dressing consisting of 6 tablespoons of oil, seasonings including a little mustard, lots of parsley, a crushed shallot and lemon juice is enough. And one could do worse than mix this sauce with a salad of cold turkey and ham or pork.

Miniatures of Calvados, or applejack, are rare but do exist. An escalope of veal fried in butter, flambéed with Calvados, the sauce enriched with cream, the whole garnished with a very small quantity of fried sweet apple, was a most attractive combination I tasted in a Rouen restaurant. With dishes like these it's the ideas that count. It isn't difficult to evolve one's own. But if you are going to flambé a dish remember always to warm the liqueur first in a spoon or ladle, or it may not light.

Some of the Christmas glacé fruits chopped and macerated in apricot liqueur or in Cointreau make a beautiful garnish for a soothing dish of cold creamed rice.

As well as brandy and the more usual liqueurs, Drambuie and a good cherry brandy are excellent comforters at this time of year.

Vin cuit is the traditional Provençal drink at Christmas and on Twelfth Night. The recipe is mentioned by the Roman writer Martial. The best-known commercial *vin cuit* is that of Palette, near Aix. Most wine growers make their own, in the following way: grape must, that is to say the unfermented juice of the grape, is put into a large copper cauldron, cooked, and skimmed, until it is reduced by one third. It is left to cool, strained, and filtered through paper. When it ceases to show any sign of throwing a deposit or of fermentation it is bottled. Sometimes a glass of *marc* or of *eau-de-vie* is added, making the wine more powerful.

WHITE LADY COCKTAIL

For Christmas entertaining, a White Lady cocktail (½ gin, ¼ Cointreau, ¼ lemon juice) makes a pleasant change from the classic Martini.

REGINA PORT COCKTAIL

The cheaper kinds of port may be made into a good mixed drink for those who do not care for gin. Regina is the port cocktail recommended by the Port Wine Growers' Association: 4 glasses of tawny port, 4 dashes of orange bitters, 1 teaspoonful of Angostura bitters, 1 teaspoonful of Cointreau. Shake well with ice, in the cocktail shaker. Float a snippet of orange peel on top of each glass.

VIN CHAUD À L'ORANGE

Among the many promising adjectives (supple, dainty, flowery, flavory, stylish, aristocratic) of the wine merchants' catalogues that make such enjoyable reading, I am sorry to see the description one of them has applied to the cheap Italian wine of which some quantity is consumed in my household: "A very big wine, almost vulgarly so." Oh dear. The slur is a little mitigated by the admission that it is a "vulgarity which can be quite welcome," and that it is suitable for cups and mulled wine. So it is. A vulgar wine is just what you want for mulling. One has learnt to dread the party at which mulled wine is served all evening, but it makes a hospitable drink to offer when guests have arrived from a cold journey, or before they set out on one. But the simpler the better. No need for a whole orchard of fruit floating in the bowl, or an East India merchant's selection of spices which makes the drink taste like liquid Christmas pudding. Try this one, with any ordinary red wine.

Tie the thinly pared rind of two oranges with thread, put it in a bowl with 4-6oz of sugar depending on what wine is used. Pour over it ¼ pint of boiling water and leave it to infuse for 15 minutes. Remove the orange peel. Pour in a bottle of red wine heated but not boiled, add the juice of the two oranges, and ladle into thick glasses.

✳ Para Navidad ✳

It is the last day of October. Here in the south-eastern corner of Spain the afternoon is hazy and the sun is warm, although not quite what it was a week ago. Then we were eating out-of-doors at midday, and were baked even in our cotton sweaters. The colors of the land are still those of late summer – roan, silver, lilac, and ochre. In the soft light the formation of the rock and the ancient terracing of the hills become clearly visible. In the summer the sun on the limestone-white soil dazzles the eyes, and the greens of June obscure the shapes of the ravines and craggy outcroppings. Now there are signs of autumn on the leaves of some of the almond trees. They have turned a frail, transparent auburn, and this morning when I awoke I devoured two of the very first tangerines of the season. In the dawn their scent was piercing and their taste was sharp. During the night it had rained – not much, nothing like enough to affect the parched soil – but all the same there was a sheen on the rose bricks and gray stones of the courtyard. The immense old terracotta oil jar in the center was freshly washed, and over the mountains a half-rainbow gave a pretty performance as we drank our breakfast coffee.

At midday we picked small figs, dusty purple and pale jade green. On the skins is a bloom not to be seen on midsummer figs. The taste, too, is quite different. The flesh is a clear garnet red, less rich and more subtle than that of the main-crop fruit, which is of the vernal variety, brilliant green. Some of the figs have split open and are half dried by the sun. In the north we can never taste fruit like this, fruit midway be-tween fresh and dried. It has the same poignancy as the black Valencia grapes still hanging in heavy bunches on the vines. These, too, are in the process of transforming themselves – from fresh grapes to raisins on the stalk as we know them. Here the bunches have been tied up in cotton bags.

The two ancients who tend the almond trees (this is Valencia almond country, and it has been a bad season. If the rain fails, next year's crop may prove to be another disaster) and who have known the estate of La Alfarella all their lives, were hoping that the grapes could be cut late and hung in the storeroom until Christmas. Their plans have been foiled by the wasps. This year there has been a fearsome plague of the persistent and destructive brutes. They have bitten their way through the protecting cotton, sucked out the juice of the fruit, and left nothing but husks. Here and there where a bunch has escaped the marauders, we have cut one and brought it back to the house in a basket with the green lemons and some of the wild thyme that has an almost overpowering scent, one that seems to be peculiar to Spanish thyme. It is perhaps fan-ciful, but it seems to have undertones of aniseed, chamomile, hyssop, lavender.

My English host, who has re-created this property of La Alfarella out of a ruin and is bringing its land back to life after twenty years of neglect, is at the cooking pots. He seizes on the green lemons and grates the skins of two of them into the meat mixture he is stirring up. He throws in a little of the sun-dried thyme and makes us a beguiling dish of *albóndigas*, little rissoles fried in olive oil. He fries them skillfully and they

emerge with a caramel-brown and gold coating reflecting the glaze of the shallow earthenware sartén, the frying dish in which they have been cooked and brought to the table. All the cooking here is done in the local earthenware pots. Even the water is boiled in them. They are very thick and sturdy, unglazed on the outside, and are used directly over the Butagaz flame, or sometimes on the wood fire in the open hearth. As yet there is no oven. That is one of next year's projects.

The kitchen is tiled in the traditional Spanish manner, deep dark blue and clean white, with a wide shelf for pots running high up along one wall. Underneath it is a row of wooden pegs on which hang the yellow pottery kitchen bowls and plate-like vegetable drainers of the district. Two holes are drilled near the rims of the bowls and sieves and a loop of string threaded through them. The earthenware pots have only loop or lug handles and there are no lids, and no stacking problem. To do duty as a cover there is always a spare pot. These cheap and practical pots make our earnest English preoccupation with the respective merits of copper, stainless steel, cast-iron and flameproof porcelain seem rather irrelevant. The same goes for our extraordinary neurosis about coffee-making devices. Here many people make their coffee in English-type aluminum boiling kettles. Spanish coffee is certainly no worse than ours – sometimes it is even hot.

Surprisingly, in an isolated farmhouse in a country believed by so many people to produce the worst and most repetitive food in Europe, our diet has a good deal of variety, and some of the produce is of a very high quality. I have never eaten such delicate and fine-grained pork meat, and the cured fillet, *lomo de cerdo*, is by any standard a luxury worth paying for. The chicken and the rabbit that go into the ritual *paella* cooked in a vast burnished iron pan (only for paella on a big scale and for the frying of *tortillas* are metal pans used) over a crackling fire are tender, possessed of their true flavors. We have had little red mullet and fresh sardines *a la plancha*, grilled on primitive round tin grill plates made sizzling hot on the fire. This is the utensil, common to France, Italy, Spain, and Greece, that also produces the best toast in the world – brittle and black-barred with the marks of the grill.

To start our midday meal we have, invariably, a tomato and onion salad, a few slices of fresh white cheese, and a dish of olives. The tomatoes are the Mediterranean ridged variety of which I never tire. They are huge, sweet, fleshy, richly red. Here they cut out and discard the central wedge, almost as we core apples, then slice the tomatoes into rough sections. They need no dressing, nothing but salt. With the roughly cut raw onions, sweet as all the vegetables grown in this limestone and clay soil, they make a wonderfully refreshing salad. It has no catchy name. It is just *ensalada*, and it cannot be reproduced without these sweet Spanish onions and Mediterranean tomatoes.

In the summer, seventeen-year-old Juanita asked for empty wine bottles to take to her married sister in the village, who would, she explained, preserve the tomatoes for the winter by slicing them, packing them in bottles, and sealing them with olive oil. They would keep for a year or more, Juanita said. Had her sister a bottle we could try? No. There were only two of last year's vintage left. They were to be kept *para Navidad*, for Christmas.

The white cheese we eat with our salad is very delicate. It is soft, but with enough body to cut into slices. It must be bought in small quantities and eaten fresh. It is made variously of cow's, ewe's, or goat's milk, and called, indiscriminately, *queso blanco*, white cheese. In the big round or oval loaves from which it is retailed it has the inviting appearance of a skillfully made pudding, chalky white, like a solidified junket marked with the lozenge pattern of the mould in which it has drained. Plastic moulds, it emerges after much questioning in the Alicante market, have replaced the traditional plaited esparto grass cheese baskets, just as plastic oil-pourers are replacing the beautiful little glass *aceiteras* which are the most practical utensil ever invented for the slow pouring out of olive oil for mayonnaise. In a hardware shop in a tiny village in the province of Jaen where we stayed the night on our way back from a journey to Portugal we were even offered a plastic mortar for mixing mayonnaise. All Spanish household plastic is made in the image of something already known and familiar, so that in a perverse and sometimes disconcerting way the plastic ware conveys a sense of continuity and tradition.

Plastic utensils the cheese makers may use – their product is real enough. Like everything we eat here it is appropriate, it belongs to the time and the place, it has an almost Arcadian freshness and innocence.

Yesterday in the market there were fresh dates from Elche, the first of the season. They are rather small, treacle-sticky, and come in tortoiseshell-cat colors: black, acorn brown, peeled-chestnut beige; like the lengths of Barcelona corduroy I have bought in the village shop. Inevitably, we were told that the best dates would not be ready until *Navidad.* That applies to the oranges and the muscatel raisins; and presumably also to the little rosy copper medlars now on sale in the market. They are not yet ripe enough to eat, so I suppose they are to be kept, like Juanita's sister's tomatoes, and the yellow and green Elche melons stored in an esparto basket in the house, for *Navidad.* We nibble at the candied melon peel in sugar-frosted and lemon-ice-colored wedges we have bought in the market, and we have already torn open the Christmas-wrapped *mazapan* (it bears the trade name of El Alce, "the elk"; a sad-faced moose with tired hooves and snow on its antlers decorates the paper), which is of a kind I have not before encountered. It is not at all like marzipan. It is very white, in bricks, with a consistency reminiscent of frozen sherbet. It is made of almonds and egg whites, and studded with crystallized fruit. There is the new season's quince cheese, the *carne de membrillo*, which we ought to be keeping to take to England for *Navidad* presents, and with it there is also a peach cheese. How is it that one never hears mention of this beautiful and delicious clear amber sweetmeat?

There are many more Mediterranean treats, cheap treats of autumn, like the newly brined green olives that the people of all olive-growing countries rightly regard as a delicacy. In Rome, one late October, I remember buying new green olives from a woman who was selling them straight from the barrel she had set up at a street corner. That was twelve years ago. I have never forgotten the fresh flavor of the Roman green olives. The *manzanilla* variety we have bought here come from Andalucía. They are neither green nor black, but purple, rose, lavender, and brown, picked at varying stages of maturity, and intended for quick home consumption rather than for export. It is the tasting of familiar products at their point of origin (before they are graded, classified, prinked up and imprisoned in bottles, tins, jars, and packets) that makes them memorable; forever changes their aspect.

By chance, saffron is another commodity that has acquired a new dimension. It was somewhere on the way up to Córdoba that we saw the first purple patches of autumn-flowering saffron crocuses in bloom. On our return we called on Mercedes, the second village girl who works at La Alfarella, to tell her that we were back. Her father was preparing saffron – picking the orange stigmas one by one from the iridescent mauve flowers heaped up in a shoe box by his side and spreading them carefully on a piece of brown paper to dry. The heap of discarded crocus petals made a splash of intense and pure color, shining like a pool of quicksilver in the cavernous shadows of the village living-room. Every night, during the six-odd weeks that the season lasts, he prepares a boxful of flowers, so his wife told us. The bundle of saffron that she took out of a battered tin, wrapped in a square of paper, and gave to us must represent a fortnight's work. It is last year's vintage because there is not yet enough of the new season's batch to make a respectable offering. It appears to have lost nothing of its penetrating, quite violently acrid-sweet and pungent scent. It is certainly a handsome present that Mercedes' mother has given us, a rare present, straight from the source, and appropriate for us to take home to England for *Navidad.*

An even better one is the rain. At last, now it is real rain that is falling. The ancient have stopped work for the day, and most of the population of the village is gathered in the café. The day the rain comes the village votes its own fiesta day.

Notes for American Cooks

The following definitions may be helpful to American cooks unfamiliar with the terminology used in Elizabeth David's writing. Note also that because of the differences in British and U.S. weights and measures (a British pint contains 20 fluid ounces, whereas the U.S. pint contains 16), the quantities given in the recipes must be considered approximate.

Ingredients

Barbados sugar	a dark raw cane sugar originally made in Barbados
Beetroot	beet
Bramley apple	an heirloom variety of apple found mainly in Europe; excellent cooking apple
Brawn	head cheese
Candy sugar	crystallized sugar
Caster sugar	superfine sugar
Chipolata	small fresh sausage
Cider	hard cider
Cos lettuce	Romaine
Cress	mustard or garden cress
Gammon	cured but uncooked ham
Hand of pork	foreleg
Haricot beans	dry white beans
Icing sugar	confectioner's sugar
Jacket potato	baked potato
Loaf sugar	conical loaf of refined sugar
Marrows	large zucchini
Orléans vinegar	fine-quality wine vinegar
Patna rice	a long-grain rice

Pig's trotters	pig's feet
Pips	seeds, usually of an apple
Prawn	shrimp
Pudding	any dessert
Rasher	slice of bacon
Salt silverside of beef	cured silverside Silverside beef, a British cut of beef from the upper side of the round; so called because of the shiny tissue on top that must be removed before cooking
Single/double cream	light/heavy cream
Sultanas	golden raisins

Equipment

Butter muslin	cheesecloth
Greaseproof paper	wax paper
Grill	broiler
Larder	pantry
Punnet	a basket or container for produce, usually berries

Measurements

Dessertspoon	2 teaspoons
Gill	¼ pint, or ½ cup
Saltspoon	¼ teaspoon
Teacup	about 5–6 ounces
Tumbler	about 6–8 ounces
Wineglass	about 4 ounces

Other

NAAFI Navy, Army and Air Force Institute, created in the UK to run recreational establishments for the British armed forces

Acknowledgments

The publishers wish to thank the following copyright-holders for permission to quote copyrighted material:

An Hour-Glass on the Run by Allan Jobson (Michael Joseph, 1959).

In Search of a Character: Two African Journals by Graham Greene (The Bodley Head, 1961). Reprinted by permission of Pollinger Limited.

A Favorite of the Gods by Sybille Bedford (Collins, 1963). Reprinted by permission of Sybille Bedford.

Salmagundi by Joyce Conyngham Green (J. M. Dent, a division of The Orion Publishing Group, 1947). Attempts to trace the copyright holder were unsuccessful.

Every effort has been made to trace or contact all copyright-holders. The publishers will be pleased to make good any omissions or rectify any mistakes brought to their attention at the earliest opportunity.

Index of Recipe Titles

Index

Index

General Index

Index

Index

Index

Index

Index

Index

Index

ELIZABETH DAVID'S CHRISTMAS
*has been set in Monotype Bell, a face based on the types cut in 1788 by Richard Austin for
John Bell's British Type Foundry. Intended for an unrealized edition of* The Book of
Common Prayer, *the types enjoyed their first substantial success as a newspaper type.
Adopted in the early twentieth century by influential American designers like D. B. Updike
and Bruce Rogers, Bell was finally issued for machine composition by Monotype in 1930,
thus ensuring the types' continued popularity.* ✳ *The extracts have been set in Quadraat, at
type designed the noted Dutch designer and type scholar, Fred Smeijers. A type designed
for digital composition, Quadraat updates Renaissance letterforms via Smeijers's
theories of type compositon and form.*

DESIGN BY SARA EISENMAN